Front cover photography and photography on pages 9, 11, 13, 15, 31, 39, 41, 43, 45, 65, 67, 69, 71, 89, 91, 93, 95, 97, 99, 111, 117, 119, 121, and 123 by Stephen Hamilton Photographics, Inc.

Photographers: Stephen Hamilton, Eric Coughlin
Photographers' Assistant: Anne Marie Zelasko
Prop Stylist: Paula Walters
Food Stylists: Josephine Orba, Maryann Melone
Assistant Food Stylists: Sheila Grannen, Jill Kaczounowski, Lisa Knych

Pictured on the front cover: Green Chicken Enchiladas (*page 122*).
Pictured on the back cover (clockwise from top): Fresh Salsa (*page 30*), Creamy Stuffed Avocado (*page 42*), and Citrus-Garlic Charbroiled Chicken (*page 120*).
Pictured on the back flap: Stuffed Poblanos in Walnut Sauce (*page 88*).

ISBN-13: 978-1-4127-2841-6
ISBN-10: 1-4127-2841-X

Manufactured in China.

8 7 6 5 4 3 2 1

Nutritional Analysis: Every effort has been made to check the accuracy of the nutritional information that appears with each recipe. However, because numerous variables account for a wide range of values for certain foods, nutritive analyses in this book should be considered approximate. Different results may be obtained by using different nutrient databases and different brand-name products.

Table of Contents

Tortillas and Egg

Chicken Tamales

Creamy Stuffed Avocado

Mexican Rice

Chef LaLa

Laura Diaz-Brown, better known in cooking circles as Chef LaLa, is a woman completely comfortable in two cultures: American and Mexican. The diminutive and dynamic Chef LaLa not only understands how Americans shop for food, cook, and eat, but is also intimately acquainted with the delicious flavors of traditional Mexican cooking.

Growing up in Los Angeles, LaLa inevitably encountered a lot of food that was labeled Mexican, but, she says, "it was not what my parents served at home or at their restaurants. They made traditional foods of Mexico: best-loved dishes from Guadalajara, where my dad grew up, and Colima, where my mom was raised." Real Mexican food, she says, bears little resemblance to Mexican fast-food, Tex-Mex, or even Southwestern cooking.

The family restaurants where LaLa honed her cooking skills were known for simple grilled meats, called *carne asada*. "The aroma of meat being grilled is instantly recognizable to anyone, and people could not resist the delicious smells," LaLa recalls. "Dad never measured anything—Mom could never tell you how long to cook a dish. They cooked entirely by feel and taste."

As a youngster, LaLa also spent summers with her *abuelita,* or "little grandmother," in Ensenada, Baja California, where they shopped daily for fresh produce and meats. "I remember delicious, fresh street foods like sliced ripe mango with chile and lime juice, and *agua de Jamaica,* a bright red tea brewed from hibiscus blossoms," LaLa recalls. "Fresh handmade tortillas were hot off the grill, and *paletas,* or ice pops, were made from fresh fruit and juices. I still remember eating a strawberry *paleta* and getting a big chunk of fresh berry in a bite."

Today, as a cookbook author, caterer, and television cooking show host, LaLa is passionate about sharing with her readers and fans the best-loved Mexican food that shaped her childhood memories and eventually influenced her career choices.

"As a Mexican-American chef, I am not so concerned about reproducing all of the authentic, regional flavors of Mexico in this book," LaLa says. "Mexico is a large country with complex cuisines representing many cultures and regions. I am more interested in sharing the best-loved Mexican food of my childhood growing up in California."

The recipes in *Best-Loved Mexican Cooking* are simple enough for busy home cooks to prepare, LaLa emphasizes. "I do not require a special chile from a certain season from a particular place in Mexico," she says. "I want to be realistic and make traditional Mexican flavors accessible for everyone. For example, if you can't find Mexican cotija cheese, a crumbly, aged white cheese that is sprinkled on tacos, soups, salads, and beans, I suggest using Greek-style feta cheese instead, which is readily available in supermarkets."

Besides making Mexican food more accessible, LaLa is also determined to put to rest the myth that Mexican food is full of fat and calories. "Fast-food Mexican chains gave rise to the idea that Mexican food is fattening and oozes yellow cheese. Not all Mexican food is deep-fried or cooked in lard. My recipes create the essence of the traditional dish without all of the extra fat. I have learned how to cut calories but not the flavor."

"If it doesn't have flavor, I don't want to eat it," says LaLa. "Flavor always plays a major role in my cooking. I am an eater first, a chef second, and a Nutritionist third. I grew up with 100% real flavors, and that is what I strive to give you in my recipes."

Tortillas and Egg

Cinnamon Apple Pancakes

Breakfast & Brunch

Divorced Eggs

Raspberry Corn Muffins

We all know that eating well in the morning adds to your energy and well-being. Enjoy these breakfast burritos, casseroles, pancakes, fruit parfaits, and other delicious ways to start every day.

Mexican-Style Sausage and Eggs

Chorizo Mexicano con Huevos

1 pound extra-lean ground pork

2 tablespoons apple cider vinegar

1½ tablespoons water

1 tablespoon ground chili powder

2 tablespoons ancho chile powder

1 tablespoon red pepper flakes

4 cloves garlic, minced

1 tablespoon dried oregano

1 teaspoon cumin seeds, crushed

1 teaspoon sugar

½ teaspoon black pepper

2½ teaspoons salt

6 eggs

1. To make sausage, place all ingredients except eggs in food processor; pulse until incorporated.

2. Heat sausage in medium skillet; use spatula to break up large pieces. Cook 4 to 5 minutes; drain. Add eggs and stir to scramble. Cook until eggs are slightly firm.

Makes 4 servings

Per Serving: 215 calories, 13g fat (4g saturated), 250mg cholesterol, 1037mg sodium, 6.3g carbohydrate (2g dietary fiber), 18.5g protein

Tip from Chef LaLa

Chorizo will keep for at least 2 weeks in the refrigerator. Place any extra chorizo in small plastic bags and freeze. Fresh chorizo can also be stuffed into casings and smoked like any other pork sausage.

Tortillas and Egg
Tortillas con Huevo

1 cup canola oil

2 corn tortillas, cut in half and sliced into medium strips

4 large eggs

Salt to taste

½ cup Fresh Salsa (see page 30)

1. Heat oil in small skillet over medium-high heat until hot but not smoking. Fry tortillas 10 to 20 seconds or until light golden and almost crisp. Transfer to paper towels; drain.

2. Whisk eggs in small bowl. Spray medium skillet with nonstick cooking spray and heat over medium-high heat. Add eggs; cook and stir until almost set, about 1 minute. Add tortilla strips. Cook and stir 1½ minutes or until egg is firm. Add salt.

3. Serve immediately with salsa.

Makes 2 servings

Per Serving (2 eggs without salsa): 224 calories, 12g fat (3g saturated), 425mg cholesterol, 166mg sodium, 13g carbohydrate (1g dietary fiber), 14g protein

Tip from Chef LaLa

For a low-fat version, bake tortilla strips instead of frying them in oil.

Green Eggs and Ham
Huevos Verdes con Jamón

8 ounces tomatillos, peeled

1 serrano chile

1 garlic clove

¼ teaspoon salt

1 teaspoon olive oil

¼ cup onion, peeled and thinly sliced

1 Anaheim chile, thinly sliced

6 ounces smoked ham, diced

4 eggs

4 Tostadas (recipe follows)

1. Place tomatillos, serrano chile and garlic in medium saucepan; cover with 1 inch water. Cook over medium heat 15 minutes; drain. Place ingredients in blender; add salt and purée.

2. Heat olive oil in large skillet over medium-high heat. Cook and stir onion and Anaheim chile 3 minutes. Add ham and cook until tender and lightly browned. Add tomatillo mixture and simmer 10 minutes.

3. Heat small skillet over medium heat; spray with nonstick cooking spray. Cooking in batches of 2, break eggs into pan 1 at a time. Cook to desired firmness.

4. Slide egg onto Tostada. Top with tomatillo and ham mixture. Serve immediately.

Makes 4 servings

Per Serving (with tostada): 298 calories, 16.4g fat (4.3g saturated), 445mg cholesterol, 809mg sodium, 15g carbohydrate (2.6g dietary fiber), 22.8g protein

Tostada
Tostada

1 cup canola oil

4 corn tortillas

Heat oil in small skillet over medium-high heat. Fry tortillas until golden brown, about 2 minutes on each side.

Makes 4 servings

Divorced Eggs
Huevos Divorciados

Tip from Chef LaLa

Drizzling sauce over the chips makes them Chilaquiles (chee-lah-KEE-lehs). This dish is popular throughout Mexico and Guatemala because it is an easy way to use stale corn tortillas. Depending on the dish, tortillas are cut into strips or broken into pieces and topped with a sauce or layered, casserole-style.

1 cup canola oil

4 corn tortillas, cut into triangles

1 cup Spicy Green Chile (see page 90)

1 cup Spicy Red Chile (see page 111)

8 large eggs

4 ounces cotija or feta cheese, crumbled

1. Heat oil in small skillet over medium-high heat until hot but not smoking. Fry tortillas in batches 10 to 20 seconds or until light golden and almost crisp. Transfer to paper towels; drain.

2. Heat green and red chile in 2 small, separate skillets.

3. Coat medium skillet with nonstick cooking spray. Cooking in batches of 2, break eggs into skillet and fry until almost set, about 1 minute. Cover to finish cooking, about 1½ minutes.

4. Transfer eggs to plate. Place tortilla chips between the eggs (the cause of the divorce!). Top 1 egg with green sauce and the other with red sauce. Drizzle extra sauce over chips. Sprinkle cheese over chips.

Makes 4 servings

Per Serving (2 eggs without chile): 382 calories, 22g fat (8g saturated), 445mg cholesterol, 723mg sodium, 20g carbohydrate (1g dietary fiber), 23g protein

Chilaquiles History

*The name **chilaquiles** is derived from the word **chil-a-quilitl**, which means "herbs or greens in chili broth" [in Nahuatl] or "a broken-up, old sombrero".*

As with most dishes there are regional versions. In Sinaloa, Mexico, the chilaquiles are prepared with a white sauce.

Mexico City is known for using a spicy tomato sauce and always tops each serving with an ample sprig of epazote.

Cinnamon Apple Pancakes
Panqueques con Canela y Manzana

1¾ cups pancake mix

¼ teaspoon ground cinnamon

1 cup water or fat-free (skim) milk

1 egg, lightly beaten, or 2 egg whites

½ cup no-sugar-added applesauce

½ cup green apples, peeled and diced

½ cup walnuts, chopped

1. Spray griddle or large skillet with nonstick cooking spray. Preheat to medium heat.

2. Combine pancake mix and cinnamon in large mixing bowl. Make a well in center of mixture. Add water, egg, applesauce, apples and walnuts. Stir with wire whisk just until blended.

3. Using ¼-cup measure or 2-ounce ladle, pour batter onto griddle. Cook pancakes on griddle until golden brown on each side, turning once.

Makes 12 pancakes

Per Serving (1 pancake): 124 calories, 3.8g fat (.4g saturated, .9g monounsaturated, 2.2g polyunsaturated), 18mg cholesterol, 285mg sodium, 18.5g carbohydrate (1.1g dietary fiber), 4.6g protein

Breakfast Burrito
Burrito para el Desayuno

¼ cup red or green bell pepper, chopped

1 green onion, sliced

6 eggs

2 tablespoons milk

¼ teaspoon salt

4 (7-inch) flour tortillas, warmed

½ cup Colby Jack or Mexican cheese blend, shredded

½ cup salsa

1. Spray skillet with nonstick cooking spray and heat over medium heat. Add bell pepper and onion; cook and stir about 3 minutes or until tender.

2. Beat eggs, milk and salt in medium bowl. Add egg mixture to skillet; reduce heat to low. Cook, stirring gently, until eggs are just set. (Eggs should be soft with no liquid remaining.)

3. Spoon one-fourth of egg mixture down center of each tortilla; top with cheese. Fold in sides to enclose filling. Serve with salsa.

Makes 4 servings

Per Serving: 273 calories, 13.6g fat (4.2g saturated), 320mg cholesterol, 502mg sodium, 25.1g carbohydrate (9.3g dietary fiber), 13.5g protein

Tip from Chef LaLa

For a healthy version of this recipe, replace whole eggs with 12 egg whites, use whole wheat tortillas instead of flour tortillas, and opt for reduced-fat cheese.

Chile Relleno Pie
Pastel de Chile Relleno

¼ cup pancake mix

3 large eggs

½ teaspoon baking powder

2 tablespoons butter

¼ cup fat-free evaporated milk

1 cup Cheddar and Monterey Jack cheese blend, shredded

½ cup canned fire-roasted whole Anaheim chiles, sliced lengthwise

Preheat oven to 350°F. Combine pancake mix, eggs, baking powder, butter and milk with a hand mixer or blender. Spray pie pan with nonstick cooking spray and sprinkle with ½ cup cheese. Pour egg mixture over cheese. Layer chiles over egg mixture and sprinkle with remaining cheese. Bake 20 minutes or until firm in center.

Makes 6 servings

Per Serving: 179 calories, 12.6g fat (7g saturated), 136mg cholesterol, 295mg sodium, 7.3g carbohydrate (2.7g dietary fiber), 8.7g protein

Mini Pumpkin Muffins
Panesitos de Calabaza

1¼ cups all-purpose flour

1 cup canned pumpkin

1 cup oatmeal

¾ cup sugar

1 tablespoon baking powder

3 eggs

1 orange, juiced

1 teaspoon ground cinnamon

⅔ cup unsweetened applesauce

½ teaspoon ground cloves

4 ounces vanilla low-fat yogurt

1. Preheat oven to 350°F. Grease mini muffin pan.

2. Combine flour, pumpkin, oatmeal, sugar, baking powder, eggs, orange juice, cinnamon, applesauce and cloves in large bowl.

3. Bake 20 to 30 minutes or until muffins are firm to the touch. Remove from oven and cool completely. Drizzle with yogurt.

Makes 12 servings

Per Serving: 200 calories, 5g fat (2.7g saturated), 54mg cholesterol, 183mg sodium, 34.3g carbohydrate (2.2g dietary fiber), 6.1g protein

Tip from Chef LaLa

*Using applesauce instead of oil
in this recipe saves 100 calories per muffin.*

Raspberry Corn Muffins
Molletes de Maíz y Frambuesa

Tip from Chef LaLa

To lower the fat in baking, substitute fruit purées, applesauce, or plain fat-free yogurt for oil.

1 cup all-purpose flour

¾ cup cornmeal

2 teaspoons baking powder

½ teaspoon baking soda

¼ teaspoon salt

1 egg, beaten

1 cup vanilla yogurt

⅓ cup frozen unsweetened apple juice concentrate, thawed

1½ cups raspberries, fresh or frozen

⅔ cup reduced-fat cream cheese

2 tablespoons raspberry fruit spread

1. Preheat oven to 350°F. Spray 12 (2½-inch) muffin cups with nonstick cooking spray.

2. Combine flour, cornmeal, baking powder, baking soda and salt in small bowl. Whisk together egg, yogurt and apple juice concentrate. Add flour mixture to egg mixture. Stir just until dry ingredients are moistened. Do not overmix. Gently stir in raspberries.

3. Spoon batter into prepared muffin cups, filling each cup three-fourths full. Bake 18 to 20 minutes or until golden brown. Let stand in pan on wire rack 5 minutes. Remove from pan; cool slightly.

4. Combine cream cheese and fruit spread in small serving bowl. Serve with warm muffins.

Makes 12 servings

Per Serving (1 muffin without topping): 98.4 calories, 1.4g fat (.6g saturated), 20mg cholesterol, 172mg sodium, 18.3g carbohydrate (1.7g dietary fiber), 3.1g protein

Seasonal Fruit and Yogurt
Fruta de Temporada con Yogurt

1 cantaloupe, peeled and seeded

1 papaya, peeled and seeded

1 small fresh pineapple, peeled, cored and cut into triangles or short spears

1½ cups strawberries, hulled and sliced, or 6 fresh figs, cut into halves

2 kiwifruit, peeled and thinly sliced

2 bananas, peeled

4 cups vanilla yogurt

8 mint sprigs (optional)

1. Cut cantaloupe and papaya into ½-inch crescents. Arrange cantaloupe, papaya, pineapple, strawberries and kiwifruit on large serving platter. Cover and chill up to 4 hours.

2. To serve, slice bananas crosswise; arrange on fruit platter. Spoon ½ cup yogurt onto plate; serve with fruit. Garnish with mint sprigs.

Makes 8 servings

Per Serving: 222 calories, 5g fat (2.5g saturated), 14mg cholesterol, 63g sodium, 43.3g carbohydrate (4.8g dietary fiber), 5.9g protein

Shredded Beef and Eggs
Machaca con Huevos

3½ cups water

1 pound beef flank steak

2 bay leaves

½ teaspoon garlic powder

1 teaspoon canola oil

1 teaspoon salt

⅛ tablespoon black pepper

1 Anaheim chile, sliced into ¼-inch pieces

1 red or green bell pepper, sliced into ¼-inch pieces

1 onion, sliced into ¼-inch pieces

8 egg whites

1. Simmer water, beef, bay leaves and garlic powder in large stock pot, covered, 2 hours or until meat is tender. Remove meat from water; allow to cool. Shred meat.

2. Heat oil in large skillet over medium heat. Add meat and cook until crispy. Add salt, pepper, chile, bell pepper and onion. Cook and stir 2 minutes or until vegetables are tender but crisp. Add egg whites and cook 5 minutes, stirring constantly until egg whites are firm. Serve immediately.

Makes 4 servings

Per Serving: 284 calories, 15g fat (6g saturated, 7g unsaturated), 74mg cholesterol, 743mg sodium, 5.8g carbohydrate (1.4g dietary fiber), 29g protein

Fresh Salsa

Apple Salsa with Cilantro and Lime

Salsas

Award Winning Salsa

Grandma's Salsa

T his familiar Mexican cuisine staple is often enjoyed as an appetizer, but salsas also can enhance any entrée, make a tasty condiment, or be served as a side to complement your main dish.

Fresh Salsa
Salsa Fresca

1½ cups tomatoes, finely chopped

¼ cup red onion,
finely chopped

2 serrano chiles, minced,
stemmed and seeds removed

1 to 2 tablespoons fresh cilantro,
shredded

½ teaspoon salt

1 teaspoon lime juice

1. Combine all ingredients in medium-sized bowl. If salsa is too hot, add more chopped tomatoes. If not hot enough, add another chile.

2. Refrigerate 30 to 60 minutes before serving, allowing flavors to combine.

Makes approximately 2 cups or 4 servings

Per Serving: 27 calories, .3g fat (0g saturated, 0g monounsaturated, 0g polyunsaturated), 0mg cholesterol, 313mg sodium, 6g carbohydrate (1.3g dietary fiber), 13g protein

Tip from Chef LaLa

Salsa, which means "sauce" in Spanish, is prepared many different ways. The most common salsa contains fresh chopped tomatoes, onions, and chiles. Use as a dip, condiment, or marinade for meats and chicken.

Apple Salsa with Cilantro and Lime

Salsa de Manzana con Cilantro y Limón

Tip from Chef LaLa

This salsa can be used to accent a meal of grilled chicken, fish, or pork.

1 cup chopped red apples

¼ cup chopped red onion

¼ cup minced Anaheim chile

½ jalapeño pepper, seeded and minced* (optional)

2 tablespoons lime juice

1 teaspoon chopped fresh cilantro

⅛ teaspoon salt

Jalapeño peppers can sting and irritate the skin, so wear rubber gloves when handling peppers and do not touch eyes.

Combine all ingredients in large bowl; mix well. Cover with plastic wrap and refrigerate at least 30 minutes or overnight.

Makes 2 cups or 8 servings

Per Serving (¼ cup): 8 calories, 0g fat (0g saturated, 0g monounsaturated, 0g polyunsaturated), 0mg cholesterol, 34mg sodium, 2.1g carbohydrate (.3g dietary fiber), .3g protein

Salsa Verde
Salsa Verde

1½ pounds tomatillos

1 serrano chile

1 clove garlic, peeled

1 tablespoon fresh cilantro, coarsely chopped

½ cup diced white onion

1 teaspoon salt

1. Peel and boil tomatillos 15 to 20 minutes. Drain and reserve ½ cup liquid.

2. Place tomatillos, serrano chile and garlic in blender. Purée until slightly chunky. Slowly incorporate liquid as needed.

3. Transfer to bowl. Add cilantro, onions and salt; mix well.

Makes 2½ cups or 10 servings

Per Serving: 32 calories, .8g fat (0g saturated, 0g unsaturated), 0mg cholesterol, 270mg sodium, 6.4g carbohydrate (1.8g dietary fiber), 1.2g protein

Tip from Chef LaLa

Although great chilled, Salsa Verde can also be served immediately, while still warm.

Tomatillos look like green tomatoes covered in papery husks. They're mainly used in salsas, especially in Salsa Verde. You can enjoy them raw or strengthen their pleasantly tart flavor by cooking them briefly.

Award Winning Salsa
Salsa Ganadora

1 red bell pepper

1 yellow bell pepper

1 green bell pepper

1 green onion, sliced

1 teaspoon olive oil

1 jalapeño pepper

1 fresno chile (yellow jalapeño)

1 red onion, diced

1 heirloom tomato, diced

1 teaspoon lime juice

2 tablespoons fresh cilantro, coarsely chopped

2 teaspoons salt

1. Heat grill to medium heat.

2. Brush bell peppers and green onion with oil. Grill bell peppers, green onion, jalapeño pepper and fresno chile until brown, but not burned, about 8 minutes. Turn frequently.

3. Peel, seed and devein peppers and chiles. Dice bell peppers, sliced green onion and chiles; place in medium bowl. Add red onion, tomato, lime juice, cilantro and salt to taste. Chill 1 hour.

Makes 3½ cups or 8 servings

Per Serving: 29 calories, .2g fat (0g saturated, 0g unsaturated), 0mg cholesterol, 238mg sodium, 6.8g carbohydrate (1.2g dietary fiber), 1g protein

Grandma's Salsa
Salsa de mi Abuelita

½ teaspoon olive oil

8 árbol chiles

1½ cups tomatoes, quartered

¼ cup onion, quartered

3 tablespoons tomato purée

½ clove garlic, peeled

1 teaspoon salt

Heat olive oil in skillet and roast chiles until brown. Transfer to blender. Add tomatoes, onion, tomato purée, garlic and salt. Purée well.

Makes 12 servings

Per Serving: 29 calories, .4g fat (0g saturated, 0g unsaturated), 0mg cholesterol, 202mg sodium, 6.3g carbohydrate (1.2g dietary fiber), 1.3g protein

Tip from Chef LaLa

Unlike many chiles, árbol chiles remain bright red even after drying. They're fairly hot. Don't confuse the dried version with the fresh; they have the same name.

Potato and Cheese Taquitos

Creamy Stuffed Avocado

Appetizers & Beverages

Beef Taquitos in Tomatillo Sauce

Chicken Tortilla Roll-Ups

Perfect for parties or for everyday snacking, these tasty, south-of-the-border small bites and beverages suit any occasion or taste. You'll enjoy the combination of authentic flavors and modern convenience.

Potato and Cheese Taquitos
Taquitos de Papa

5 cups boiled potatoes, peeled and diced

1 cup grated Monterey Jack or Gouda cheese

3 green onions, finely chopped

1 teaspoon salt

1 teaspoon black pepper

24 corn tortillas

1 cup canola or vegetable oil

Mango Guacamole (recipe follows)

1. Combine cooked potatoes, cheese, onions, salt and pepper in large mixing bowl.

2. Warm tortillas to soften. Place 1 tablespoon filling in a narrow strip at one end of each tortilla. Roll up tightly; secure in center with a wooden toothpick. Heat oil until hot in medium skillet. Fry in batches, several taquitos at a time until crisp.

3. Drain taquitos on paper towels. Remove toothpicks and serve immediately. Top with Mango Guacamole.

Makes 4 servings

Per Serving (1 taquito): 117 calories, 4.4g fat (1.1g saturated, 1.9g monounsaturated, 1.0g polyunsaturated), 4mg cholesterol, 112g sodium, 17.2g carbohydrate (1.9g dietary fiber), 3.3g protein

Mango Guacamole

2 cups mango, diced

1 cup chopped tomatoes

2 tablespoons chopped fresh cilantro

½ cup finely diced red onion

3 serrano chiles, finely diced

1 large avocado, finely diced

Juice of ½ lime

1 teaspoon salt

Combine all ingredients in medium bowl. Stir to combine.

Makes 4 cups

Per ⅓-cup Serving: 58 calories, .2g fat (.4g saturated, 1.6g monounsaturated, .4g polyunsaturated), 0mg cholesterol, 183mg sodium, 9.3g carbohydrate (2.5g dietary fiber), 1g protein

Scallop Drunk Balls
Concha de Peregrino Bolitas Borachas

1 pound small bay scallops

⅔ cup lime juice

½ teaspoon salt

½ cup honeydew melon, balled

½ cup cantaloupe, balled

½ cup watermelon, balled

2 tablespoons tequila

6 large fresh mint leaves, cut chiffonade-style

Additional fresh mint leaves (optional)

1. Combine scallops, lime juice and salt in medium bowl. Refrigerate 30 minutes.

2. Combine scallop mixture, melon balls, tequila and mint. Stir to combine. Refrigerate 15 minutes. Serve in decorative dish or glass. Garnish with additional mint.

Makes 4 servings

Per 1-cup Serving: 156 calories, 1.2g fat (.1g saturated, 0g monounsaturated, .3g polyunsaturated), 37g cholesterol, 458g sodium, 13.4g carbohydrate (.9g dietary fiber), 20g protein

Tip from Chef LaLa

"Chiffonade" means to cut leaves into tiny ribbons.

Creamy Stuffed Avocado
Aguacate Cremoso Relleno

Tip from Chef LaLa

For a variation, replace chicken with 10 ounces cooked and peeled small salad shrimp.

For a vegetarian version, replace chicken with 16 ounces frozen mixed vegetables (carrots, peas, corn, green beans, lima beans), rinsed and thawed.

1 pound boneless, skinless chicken breasts

1 stalk celery

¼ cup chopped onion

2 tablespoons light mayonnaise

1 tablespoon light sour cream

½ cup finely shredded iceberg lettuce

¼ cup diced celery

½ teaspoon celery salt

6 ounces small frozen peas, thawed

White pepper to taste

5 medium avocados, ripe, firm

Lemon juice or olive oil

Celery salt to taste

Purple chard or red lettuce

Paprika

1. Place chicken breast, celery stalk and onion into medium pot and bring to boil. Reduce heat and simmer 1 hour. Remove chicken. Strain and discard vegetables. Shred chicken. (Note: Chicken will be approximately 10 ounces cooked.)

2. Combine mayonnaise, sour cream, lettuce, celery, celery salt, peas and white pepper in medium bowl. Stir well. Add shredded chicken; mix thoroughly. Adjust seasonings to taste.

3. Cut avocados in half lengthwise and remove pit. Peel and trim a little off the bottom so that the half sits upright. Brush with lemon juice or olive oil. Lightly sprinkle with celery salt.

4. Scoop ¼ cup chicken mixture into each avocado half. Place avocado onto plate with bed of purple chard or red lettuce. Sprinkle with paprika.

Makes 10 servings

Per Serving: 227 calories, 18.9g fat (2.7g saturated, 9.8g monounsaturated, 2.1g polyunsaturated), 21mg cholesterol, 161mg sodium, 10.5g carbohydrate (7g dietary fiber), 11.5g protein

Beef Taquitos in Tomatillo Sauce
Taquitos de Res en Salsa de Tomatillo

Tip from Chef LaLa

Taquitos are great as an appetizer or meal.

Filling

1 pound flank steak, cooked and shredded

6 cups water

1 small onion, quartered

2 cloves garlic, peeled

2 bay leaves

5 black peppercorns

1 teaspoon salt

Sauce

4 cups crushed tomatillos, canned or fresh

1 medium onion

1 medium Anaheim chile

½ medium green bell pepper

2 cloves garlic

1 tostada (see page 12)

3 ounces canned jalapeño peppers (optional)

¼ cup chopped fresh cilantro

Taquitos

20 corn tortillas

1 cup oil

¼ cup crema fresca, sour cream or crème fraîche

1 medium avocado, sliced

4 ounces cotija cheese, crumbled

1. Simmer steak, water, onion, garlic, bay leaves and peppercorns in large pot 2 hours or until meat is tender. Add salt and additional water if needed; cook 15 minutes more. Remove and discard bay leaves. Remove meat and reserve liquid. Cool and shred meat.

2. Purée tomatillos, onion, chile, bell pepper, garlic, tostada, jalapeños and reserved liquid in blender or food processor. Add cilantro and process briefly until smooth.

3. Heat tortillas on griddle on medium heat until pliable. Fill with thin strip of meat lengthwise and roll tortillas tightly. Secure with wooden toothpicks.

4. Fill large skillet with ½ inch oil; heat over medium-high heat. Fry taquitos 3 to 4 minutes or until crisp and golden brown on all sides. Remove taquitos from pan and drain on paper towels. Wipe off excess oil and remove toothpicks.

5. Serve with tomatillo sauce; top with crema fresca, avocado and cheese.

Makes 20 taquitos

Per Serving (1 taquito with sauce and garnish): 170 calories, 9g fat (2g saturated, 3.8g monounsaturated, 1.2g polyunsaturated), 16mg cholesterol, 493mg sodium, 14g carbohydrate (2.6g dietary fiber), 8g protein

Jalapeño Cheese Crisps
Tostaditas de Jalapeño y Queso

1½ cups all-purpose flour

½ cup yellow cornmeal

½ teaspoon sugar

1 teaspoon salt

½ teaspoon baking soda

½ cup (1 stick) butter or butter with canola blend

1½ cups sharp Cheddar cheese, shredded (6 ounces)

2 tablespoons juice from canned jalapeño peppers

½ cup cold water

Black pepper and salt to taste

1. Combine flour, cornmeal, sugar, salt and baking soda in large bowl. Cut in butter with pastry blender or two knives until mixture resembles coarse crumbs. Stir in cheese, jalapeño juice and water with fork until soft dough forms. Cover and refrigerate 1 hour or freeze 30 minutes until firm.*

2. Preheat oven to 375°F. Grease 2 baking sheets. Divide dough into 4 pieces. Roll each piece on floured surface into paper-thin circle, about 13 inches in diameter.

3. Cut each circle into 8 wedges; place on prepared baking sheets. Bake about 12 minutes or until crisp. Sprinkle with salt and pepper. Store in airtight container up to 3 days.

*Dough may be frozen at this point. Thaw in refrigerator and proceed as directed.

Makes 32 crisps

Per Serving (4 crisps): 394 calories, 19.5g fat (12g saturated, 5.5g monounsaturated, .8g polyunsaturated), 5.5mg cholesterol, 600mg sodium, 28.2g carbohydrate (.6g dietary fiber), 9g protein

Oysters Cotija
Ostiones Cotija

12 oysters, shucked and on the half shell

2 slices bacon, cut into 12 (1-inch) pieces

½ cup unseasoned dry bread crumbs

2 tablespoons butter, melted

¼ teaspoon garlic powder

⅛ teaspoon ground árbol chiles or paprika

1 ounce cotija, Romano or Parmesan cheese, grated

2 tablespoons chopped fresh cilantro, minced (optional)

1. Preheat oven to 375°F. Place shells with oysters on baking sheet. Top each oyster with 1 piece bacon. Bake 10 minutes or until bacon is crisp.

2. Meanwhile, combine bread crumbs, butter, garlic powder and ground chile in small bowl. Spoon mixture over oysters; sprinkle with cheese. Bake 5 to 10 minutes. Garnish with cilantro.

Makes 12 appetizers

Per Serving (1 oyster): 60 calories, 3.7g fat (2g saturated, 1g monounsaturated, .7g polyunsaturated), 15mg cholesterol, 134mg sodium, 4g carbohydrate (.3g dietary fiber), 2.5g protein

Tip from Chef LaLa

Oysters are a well-balanced food because they contain protein, carbohydrates, and lipids, and are a good source of vitamins A, B1 (thiamin), B2 (riboflavin), B3 (niacin), C (ascorbic acid) and D (calciferol). 4 or 5 oysters supply the recommended daily allowance of iron, copper, iodine, magnesium, calcium, zinc, manganese and phosphorus.

Applewood bacon works well in this recipe.

Chicken Tortilla Roll-Ups
Rollitos de Pollo

1 cup chicken, cooked, finely chopped

2 tablespoons reduced-fat mayonnaise

¼ teaspoon celery salt

¼ teaspoon black pepper

1 tablespoon green onion, chopped

6 jalapeño or white cheese slices

3 (10- or 12-inch) wheat or flour tortillas

¼ cup carrot, shredded or finely chopped

¼ cup fresh or canned roasted jalapeño pepper, finely chopped

½ cup lettuce, finely shredded

1. Combine chicken, mayonnaise, celery salt, black pepper and green onion in small bowl; stir until well blended.

2. Place cheese slices onto each tortilla, leaving ½-inch border. Spread a thin layer of chicken mixture, carrot, peppers and lettuce evenly over cheese.

3. Roll up each tortilla jelly-roll fashion. Cut each roll into 4 to 5 slices.

Makes 12 slices or 6 servings

Per Serving (with wheat tortilla): 521 calories, 36g fat (21g saturated, 10g monounsaturated, 2g polyunsaturated), 118mg cholesterol, 733mg sodium, 15g carbohydrate (4.5g dietary fiber), 37g protein

Tip from Chef LaLa

Wrap rolls in plastic wrap and refrigerate for several hours for easier slicing.

Placing cheese directly on the tortilla before the chicken mixture prevents the moisture of the chicken from making the tortilla soggy.

For a lighter version, use reduced-fat cheese.

Chipotle Chicken Bundles
Paquetes de Pollo en Chipotle

Tip from Chef LaLa

This recipe also tastes great with ground turkey.

3 tablespoons soy sauce

½ tablespoon cornstarch

1 tablespoon extra-virgin olive oil

2 cloves garlic, minced

1 pound ground chicken

⅓ cup jícama, diced

⅓ cup green onions, thinly sliced

¼ cup peanuts, chopped

2 tablespoons canned chipotle jalapeño in adobo sauce

12 large lettuce leaves

1. Mix soy sauce with cornstarch in cup until smooth.

2. Heat oil in large skillet over medium-high heat. Add garlic and cook 1 minute. Add chicken; cook and stir 2 to 3 minutes or until chicken is cooked through.

3. Stir soy sauce mixture and add to pan. Stir-fry 2 minutes or until sauce boils and thickens. Remove from heat, stir in jícama, green onions, peanuts and adobo sauce.*

4. Divide filling evenly among lettuce leaves; roll up. Tie closed with chive or green onion. Serve warm or at room temperature. Do not let filling stand at room temperature more than 2 hours.

*Note: Filling may be made ahead to this point; cover and refrigerate up to 4 hours. Reheat chicken filling until warm. Proceed as directed in step 4.

Makes 12 appetizers

Per Serving (with ground turkey): 117 calories, 6.1g fat (1.3g saturated, 2.8g monounsaturated, 1.4g polyunsaturated), 36mg cholesterol, 243mg sodium, 2.7g carbohydrate (.7g dietary fiber), 12.8g protein

Guacamole and Cucumber Chips

Guacamole con Tostones de Pepino

2 large avocados, ripe

½ cup green onions, minced

1½ serrano chiles, seeded, minced

1½ tablespoons fresh cilantro, finely chopped

½ medium tomato, seeded and diced

1 teaspoon lime juice

½ teaspoon salt

¼ cup water

2 English or hot house cucumbers, sliced

1. Cut avocados in half; remove and reserve pits. Make small squares with small knife in avocado flash. Scoop flesh into medium bowl.

2. Add green onions, serrano chiles, cilantro, tomato, lime juice, salt and water. Fold ingredients to combine.

3. Transfer guacamole to serving bowl. Serve with cucumber "chips."

Makes 8 servings

Per Serving: 96.2 calories, 7.8g fat (1.3g saturated, 4.8g monounsaturated, 1g polyunsaturated), 0mg cholesterol, 142mg sodium, 7g carbohydrate (3.8g dietary fiber), 2g protein

Tip from Chef LaLa

Dicing and folding avocados while mixing are both important elements in preventing guacamole from looking "muddy."

Place the avocado pits in the guacamole bowl to help prevent it from turning brown.

Lobster, Squid and Shrimp Citrus Ceviche

Ceviche Cítrico de Langosta, Calamar y Camarón

Tip from Chef LaLa

Don't overcook the lobster; it will become chewy.

½ pound raw shrimp, shelled (16 to 20 count)

½ cup freshly squeezed lime juice

1 medium jalapeño pepper, seeded, cut into very thin slices lengthwise*

¼ cup red onion, diced

8 ounces lobster tail, fresh or frozen and defrosted

1 cup water

½ cup lime juice

¼ cup white wine

10 squid, cleaned and cut into rings and tentacles

Ice cubes

½ cup fresh orange juice

3 tablespoons chopped fresh cilantro

½ medium cucumber, peeled, seeded and diced

Jalapeño peppers can sting and irritate the skin, so wear rubber gloves when handling peppers and do not touch eyes.

1. Clean and devein shrimp. Combine shrimp, lime juice, jalapeño and onion in medium glass bowl. Refrigerate 1 hour.

2. Remove lobster meat from shell and chop into medium pieces. In small saucepan, combine water, lime juice and wine; bring to a simmer. Add meat; cook 3 minutes or until tender. Add squid; cook 30 seconds or until opaque; drain. Add a few ice cubes to cool; drain. Place lobster, squid and orange juice in small bowl; refrigerate 30 minutes.

3. Combine shrimp, lobster, squid and juice mixture in medium bowl. Add cilantro and cucumber. Stir to combine and refrigerate 30 minutes before serving.

Makes 6 appetizer servings

Per Serving: 242 calories, 3g fat (.7g saturated, .4g monounsaturated, 1g polyunsaturated), 424mg cholesterol, 236mg sodium, 13g carbohydrate (1g dietary fiber), 38g protein

Tamarind Drink
Agua de Tamarindo

25 tamarind pods	1½ cups sugar
1 gallon water	Ice cubes

The tamarind, also called an Indian date, is the fruit of tall shade trees native to Asia and northern Africa. They were brought to Mexico from India and have spread to Central America. Tamarind pods resemble large, brown beans. The fruit is tart and has fibrous flesh and a flat stone in the center.

1. Peel tamarind. Pour 1 gallon boiling water over tamarind in large mixing bowl; add sugar. Soak 45 minutes, stirring often to dissolve the sugar and tamarind pulp.

2. Strain through sieve into pitcher with ice. Chill. Serve with ice.

Makes 16 servings

Per Serving: 80 calories, 0g fat (0g saturated, 0g unsaturated), 0mg cholesterol, 8mg sodium, 20g carbohydrate (.2g dietary fiber), .1g protein

Slushy Piña Colada
Piña Colada

1 cup fresh pineapple, diced	2 cups ice cubes
¼ cup water	Sugar (optional)
¼ cup coconut cream	Fresh mint sprigs (optional)
6 ounces light rum	

Place pineapple and water in blender; blend until smooth. Add coconut cream, light rum and ice cubes. Blend until slushy. Add sugar, if desired. Garnish with mint sprigs.

Makes 1 quart

Per Serving: 164 calories, 5.1g fat (4.4g saturated, .2g monounsaturated, .1g polyunsaturated), 0mg cholesterol, 5mg sodium, 5.7g carbohydrate (.5g dietary fiber), .7g protein

Tip from Chef LaLa

The pineapple season is March through July. When buying fresh pineapple, make sure there are no signs of greening. The leaves should be crisp and green with no yellow or brown spots. The skin of the pineapple should give slightly to pressure. Soft or dark spots are indications of over-ripening.

Blood Orange Raspado
Raspado de Naranja

¾ cup water

¾ cup sugar

2 cups blood orange juice*

⅛ teaspoon red food coloring (optional)

⅛ teaspoon yellow food coloring (optional)

Whole, fresh strawberries (optional)

1. Combine water and sugar in medium saucepan. Bring to a boil. Lower heat to simmer; add orange juice. Stir to dissolve sugar. Add food colorings, if desired.

2. Transfer juice mixture to shallow pan and place in freezer. Stir with a fork every 30 minutes. Continue to freeze, stirring occasionally to break up ice crystals until completely frozen, about 3 hours. Garnish with strawberries.

Makes 4 servings

If blood oranges are not available, use naval oranges instead.

Per Serving: 201 calories, .3g fat (0g saturated, .1g monounsaturated, .1g polyunsaturated), 0mg cholesterol, 3mg sodium, 50g carbohydrate (.3g dietary fiber), .9g protein

Citrus Chipotle Skewers

Alambres de Pollo en Chipotle Citrico

3 pounds boneless, skinless chicken breasts

48 metal or bamboo skewers

7 ounces chipotle peppers in adobe sauce

1 pint (16 ounces) frozen orange juice

½ cup tangerine juice

⅓ cup sliced onion

4 cloves garlic, minced

¼ teaspoon black pepper

4 tablespoons olive oil

1 tablespoon salt

Orange slices (optional)

1. Cut chicken breasts into diagonal strips, ½ to 1 inch thick. Each skewer should weigh approximately 1.5 ounces. Thread chicken onto skewers. Place skewers in bowl.

2. Remove chipotle peppers from sauce; coarsely chop. Set aside; reserve sauce.

3. Combine juices, onion, garlic, pepper, olive oil, chopped chipotle peppers and remaining adobe sauce (reserving some sauce for garnish) in large bowl.

4. Pour mixture over skewers and marinate in refrigerator 2 to 4 hours. Add salt to marinade just before cooking.

5. Grill skewers over medium heat 3 minutes on each side or until desired doneness. Garnish with orange slices and drizzle with reserved adobe sauce.

Makes 8 servings or 48 skewers

Per Serving: 209 calories, 1.6g fat (.4g saturated, 1.2g unsaturated), 65mg cholesterol, 182mg sodium, 20.6g carbohydrate (1.1g dietary fiber), 27.6g protein

Tip from Chef LaLa

The acidity in the citrus juices tenderizes the chicken. Marinating (overnight) can produce a better result.

Skewers are excellent as an appetizer or an entrée.

Mexican Rice

Refried Beans

Soups, Salads & Sides

Tortilla Soup

Colorful Cabbage Slaw

Hot, steamy bowls of soup and light, crisp salads go hand-in-hand all year long. Enjoy them on their own or paired with a delicious side dish for a complete, satisfying meal.

Red Pozole with Chicken and Pork
Pozole Rojo con Pollo y Puerco

Tip from Chef LaLa

Leaving the meat on the bones during the cooking process adds more flavor to the pozole.

Skimming the pozole removes approximately ¼ cup of fat.

Pozole is a staple of Mexican cuisine. Each region offers several variations. The name pozole refers to whole-kernel hominy, or large kernels of dried corn that have been soaked in lime juice to remove outer skins and puff them up.

2 pounds pork neck bones with meat

3 to 4 pounds fresh whole skinless chicken, cut into pieces

¼ cup canola oil

1 large onion, chopped

4 cloves garlic, minced

16 cups (1 gallon) chicken broth or water

3 dried guajillo chiles, toasted

3 dried pasilla chiles, toasted

1 cup water

10 cups canned hominy maíz, drained

2 teaspoons salt

Shredded cabbage, chopped onions, dried oregano, lime wedges and tostadas (see page 12)

1. Wash pork bones and chicken. Heat large pot over medium-high heat; add oil and cook pork bones and chicken, skin-side-down, until browned. Remove chicken and pork bones; set aside.

2. Drain excess oil from pot, leaving only enough to coat the pot. Add onion; cook, stirring constantly until translucent, about 5 minutes. Add garlic; cook 2 minutes more.

3. Return chicken and pork bones to pot and cover with chicken broth. Skim off any foam that rises to surface; cover and reduce heat to simmer. Cook 2½ to 3 hours or until pork is tender.

4. While meat is cooking, remove seeds and veins from dried chiles. Soak in boiling water 20 minutes. Drain and purée chiles with 1 cup water in blender. Set aside.

5. Remove chicken and pork bones from pot. Cool slightly and shred meat, removing and discarding bones. Return chicken and pork to pot, skimming off any foam that has accumulated.

6. Add hominy and chile purée to pot; simmer about 1 hour or until slightly thickened. Add salt and additional water if needed.

7. Serve in shallow bowls with shredded cabbage, onions, pinch of dry oregano, lime wedges and tostadas on the side.

Makes 16 servings

Per Serving: 260 calories, 12.2g fat (2.7g saturated, 5.4g monounsaturated, 3g polyunsaturated), 68mg cholesterol, 539mg sodium, 13g carbohydrate (2.2g dietary fiber), 23.3g protein

Mexican Rice
Arroz Mexicano

8 ounces canned tomato sauce

¼ medium onion

1 clove garlic

2 cups unsalted chicken broth, divided

1 cup long grain white rice

2 tablespoons canola oil

1 tablespoon salt

½ cup frozen peas and carrots

1. Blend tomato sauce, onion, garlic and ¼ cup chicken broth in blender or food processor until smooth. Set aside.

2. Wash rice thoroughly until water runs clear; drain.

3. Heat oil in medium skillet over medium-high heat. Add rice; stir occasionally until golden brown. Add tomato mixture; cook until tomato sauce starts to brown, about 10 minutes. Add remaining 1½ cups chicken stock and salt; bring to a boil. Add frozen peas and carrots. Cover; lower heat and cook 15 minutes or until tender.

Makes 3 cups or 6 servings

Per Serving: 141 calories, 4.7g fat (.6g saturated, 2.7g monounsaturated, 1g polyunsaturated), 0mg cholesterol, 621mg sodium, 24g carbohydrate (1.2g dietary fiber), 1g protein

Tortilla Soup
Sopa de Tortilla

2 boneless, skinless chicken breasts

½ medium onion, chopped

2 medium carrots, chopped

2 stalks celery, chopped

1½ cups chicken broth

8 cups water

3 dried guajillo chiles, toasted*

2 cups hot water

½ cup canola oil

5 corn tortillas

3 tablespoons canola oil

2 cloves garlic, minced

½ small onion, chopped

3 ounces canned tomato paste

1 teaspoon salt

2 ears white corn kernels

1 medium tomato, chopped

3 ounces queso fresco

½ avocado, chopped

¼ cup chopped fresh cilantro

If guajillo chiles cannot be found, try substituting New Mexico or California chiles (milder).

1. Cook chicken, onion, carrots, celery, broth and water in large pot 30 to 45 minutes over medium heat. Remove chicken and shred. Strain and reserve liquid, discarding vegetables.

2. Soak chiles in hot water 20 minutes. Remove seeds and tops. Drain when soft; discard liquid.

3. Heat ½ cup oil in medium frying pan to 360°F. Cut 3 tortillas into thin strips. Fry strips until golden brown. Remove; drain well. Fry an additional 2 tortillas whole; drain.

4. Place 2 whole fried tortillas in blender with chiles and 2 cups reserved liquid; blend until smooth.

5. Heat 3 tablespoons oil in large pot over medium heat. Add garlic and onion; cook until soft. Add tomato paste and cook until just brown. Add blended chile mixture, remaining reserved liquid, salt and corn. Cook 15 minutes.

6. Place one-sixth of shredded chicken in bowl. Ladle liquid over chicken. Top with tortilla strips, tomato, queso fresco, avocado and cilantro.

Makes 6 servings

Per Serving: 334 calories, 10.8g fat (2.1g saturated, 4.8g monounsaturated, 2.8g polyunsaturated), 48mg cholesterol, 881mg sodium, 37g carbohydrate (4g dietary fiber), 24.3g protein

Refried Beans
Frijoles Refritos

2 cups dried pinto beans

10 cups water

1 teaspoon salt

3 tablespoons canola oil

1 ounce cotija or queso fresco cheese, crumbled (optional)

1. Rinse, drain and soak beans overnight.

2. Add 10 cups water to beans. Cover and cook 2 hours over medium heat. Add additional water, if needed. Add salt; cook 15 minutes more or until beans are soft and skins are just beginning to break open.

3. Heat oil in large skillet over medium-high heat. Add beans and liquid. Using a potato masher, mash beans in skillet while cooking until they are a rough purée. (Add more water if too dry or cook longer to dry out if consistency is too watery.) Garnish with cotija or queso fresco cheese.

Makes 12 servings

Per Serving: 172 calories, 6.4g fat (2g saturated, 2.1g monounsaturated, 1.1g polyunsaturated) 7mg cholesterol, 324mg sodium, 20g carbohydrate (7.9g dietary fiber), 9.1g protein

---

Tip from Chef LaLa

"Refried" is actually deceptive. Refritos means "fried," not "refried," though you can certainly reheat the beans as you go through a batch.

Note that when multiplying the recipe, cooking time will vary depending on the batch of beans you have.

To save 30 calories per serving, omit the oil and smash the beans in the skillet.

Beef Fajita Soup
Sopa de Fajitas de Res

1 tablespoon vegetable
or canola oil

1 pound skirt steak, trimmed,
sliced

1 small onion, thinly sliced

1 clove garlic

1 can (15 ounces) pinto beans,
rinsed and drained

1 can (15 ounces) black beans,
rinsed and drained

1 small green bell pepper, thinly
sliced

1 small red bell pepper, thinly
sliced

1 can (14½ ounces) beef broth

1 cup water

⅛ teaspoon black pepper

Heat oil in large skillet over medium-high heat. Brown and stir steak
5 minutes. Add onion and garlic; cook 3 minutes more. Transfer to large pot.
Add beans, bell peppers, beef broth, water and black pepper. Lower heat; cover
and simmer 30 to 45 minutes or until meat is tender.

Makes 8 servings

Per Serving: 502 calories, 9.6g fat (3.2g saturated, 3.9g monounsaturated, 1.3g polyunsaturated),
29mg cholesterol, 506mg sodium, 693g carbohydrate (21.7g dietary fiber), 36.2g protein

---

Tip from Chef LaLa

*Cooking times for meat vary and depend on skillet size
and weight, quality of meat and type of stove. Always taste
meat before serving. If tough, it will become more tender when
cooked longer. Also add any additional salt at the end. As liquid
evaporates, the overall flavor and saltiness changes.*

Freshly cooked beans are great in this recipe as well.

Sweet and Spicy Salad
Ensalada Dulce y Picosita

Tip from Chef LaLa

Salad with vinegar shows the influence of early European explorers in Mexico and the mingling of New and Old World flavors.

Dressing

- 1 cup fresh raspberries
- 1 cup balsamic vinegar
- 1½ tablespoons sugar

Salad

- 10 cups packed mesclun or mixed torn lettuce
- 4 ounces queso fresco or goat cheese, crumbled
- ½ cup dried cranberries
- ½ cup Sweet and Spicy Cayenne Nuts (see page 85), walnuts or pecans, coarsely chopped and toasted*

*To toast nuts, spread in single layer on baking sheet. Bake in preheated 350°F oven 8 to 10 minutes or until golden brown, stirring frequently.

1. To make dressing, mash raspberries with fork in small bowl. Whisk in balsamic vinegar and sugar.

2. For salad, combine salad greens, queso fresco, cranberries and nuts in large bowl. Whisk dressing again and add to salad; toss until evenly coated.

Makes 8 servings

Per Serving: 126 calories, 6.1g fat (1.2g saturated, 3.2g monounsaturated, 1.3g polyunsaturated), 5mg cholesterol, 26mg sodium, 17.5g carbohydrate (3.3g dietary fiber), 3.6g protein

Colorful Cabbage Slaw

Ensalada de Repollo Colorido

1 (6-inch) corn tortilla, cut into thin strips

¼ teaspoon chili powder

¼ teaspoon salt

3 cups shredded green cabbage

1 cup shredded red cabbage

½ cup shredded carrots

½ cup sliced radishes

½ cup canned corn, drained

¼ cup chopped fresh cilantro

½ tablespoon dried oregano

½ tablespoon brown sugar

¼ cup olive oil

½ tablespoon onion powder

½ cup apple cider vinegar

½ teaspoon garlic salt

¼ teaspoon black pepper

¼ teaspoon salt

½ cup unsalted roasted peanuts

1. Preheat oven to 350°F. Arrange tortilla strips in even layer on nonstick baking sheet. Spray strips with nonstick cooking spray and sprinkle with chili powder and salt. Bake 6 to 8 minutes or until strips are crisp.

2. Combine cabbage, carrots, radishes, corn and cilantro in large bowl. Combine oregano, brown sugar, olive oil, onion powder, apple cider vinegar, garlic salt, black pepper, salt and peanuts in separate bowl.

3. Add vinegar mixture to cabbage mixture; toss gently to coat. Marinate in refrigerator 2 hours. Serve topped with baked tortilla strips.

Makes 8 servings

Per Serving: 155 calories, 11.6g fat (1.6g saturated, 7.2g monounsaturated, 2.1g polyunsaturated), 0mg cholesterol, 155mg sodium, 11.7g carbohydrate (2g dietary fiber), 3.7g protein

Gazpacho Salad
Ensalada de Gazpacho

Tip from Chef LaLa

To peel tomatoes easily, blanch in boiling water for 30 seconds; immediately transfer to a bowl of cold water and then peel.

½ cup peeled and coarsely chopped tomato

1 cup peeled, seeded and chopped cucumber

¾ cup chopped onion

½ cup finely chopped red bell pepper

½ cup fresh or frozen corn, cooked and drained

¼ cup fresh lime juice

1 tablespoon red wine vinegar

2 teaspoons water

1 teaspoon extra-virgin olive oil

1 teaspoon fresh garlic, minced

½ teaspoon salt

¼ teaspoon white pepper

Pinch ground red pepper

1 medium head romaine lettuce, torn into bite-size pieces

1 cup peeled and diced jícama

½ cup fresh cilantro sprigs

1. Combine tomato, cucumber, onion, bell pepper and corn in large bowl. Combine lime juice, vinegar, water, oil, garlic, salt, white pepper and ground red pepper in small bowl; whisk until well blended. Pour over tomato mixture; toss well. Cover and refrigerate several hours to allow flavors to blend.

2. Toss together lettuce, jícama and cilantro in another large bowl. Divide lettuce mixture evenly among 6 plates. Place ⅔ cup chilled tomato mixture on top of lettuce, spreading to edges.

Makes 6 servings

Per Serving: 47 calories, 1.1g fat (.1g saturated, .6g monounsaturated, .2g polyunsaturated), 0mg cholesterol, 260mg sodium, 9.5g carbohydrate (2.3g dietary fiber), 1.6g protein

Prickly Salad
Ensalada de Nopalitos

1 cup fresh or canned nopales, sliced

1 small red onion, thinly sliced

3 tablespoons apple cider vinegar

4 tablespoons finely chopped fresh cilantro

½ teaspoon minced fresh oregano

½ cup cotija cheese, crumbled (about 12 ounces)

1 teaspoon olive oil

4 medium tomatoes, chopped

1 head romaine lettuce

5 radishes, thinly sliced

1 large ripe, firm avocado, peeled and sliced

1. Combine nopales, onion, vinegar, cilantro and oregano in large bowl. Marinate 15 to 30 minutes.

2. Add cotija cheese, olive oil and tomatoes to mixture.

3. Arrange lettuce around rim of large serving platter. Transfer mixture to platter in center of lettuce. Garnish with radish and avocado.

Makes 5 servings or 5 cups

Per Serving: 123 calories, 7.6g fat (1.6g saturated, 0g unsaturated), 4mg cholesterol, 145mg sodium, 12.6g carbohydrate (5.8g dietary fiber), 4.4g protein

Cheese and Mango Salad
Ensalada de Mango y Queso

- 2 ounces queso fresco
- 1 tablespoon shredded fresh cilantro
- 1 tablespoon lime juice
- ¼ cup chopped red onion
- 1 teaspoon extra-virgin olive oil
- ⅓ cup sliced tomato
- ⅓ cup sliced English or hot house cucumber
- ½ cup peeled and sliced mango

Combine all ingredients in large mixing bowl. Gently toss. Chill 1 hour. Serve on decorative plate.

Makes 2 servings

Per Serving: 122 calories, 5g fat (1.8g saturated, 3.2g unsaturated), 16.6mg cholesterol, 150mg sodium, 16.6g carbohydrate (2.3g dietary fiber), 4.8g protein

Tip from Chef LaLa

All citrus fruits, such as limón (lime), are rich in vitamin C as well as other micro-nutrients, certain phytochemicals and fiber. Citrus fruits also protect against infection and cancer. They are an essential element in any healthy diet.

Mexican Squash with Corn
Calabasitas con Elote

Tip from Chef LaLa

Squash is native to the western hemisphere with origins in Latin America as far back as 5500 BC. Mexican squash may be round or elongated, is green with white stripes on the skin and has a soft, fleshy interior. Select firm, plump, and unblemished squash.

¾ cup seeded and chopped tomato

1 cup Mexican squash, cut into ½-inch-thick slices

4 ounces canned corn, drained

2 ounces Monterey Jack cheese, sliced

Baking Method

1. Preheat oven to 375°F.

2. Place tomato, squash and corn in baking dish. Top with cheese. Bake 15 minutes.

Stove Top Method

1. Place tomato, squash and corn in large skillet. Cook over medium to high heat 5 minutes, stirring occasionally. (Vegetables should be firm, not mushy.)

2. Top with cheese; cover. Cook 3 minutes to melt cheese or place in broiler to brown cheese.

Makes 3 servings

Per Serving: 69 calories, 2g fat (1.1g saturated, .9g unsaturated), 6mg cholesterol, 481mg sodium, 10.6g carbohydrate (1.6g dietary fiber), 4.2g protein

Sweet and Spicy Cayenne Nuts
Nueces Dulces y Picositos

2 cups pecan halves

2 teaspoons chili powder

1 tablespoon ground red (cayenne) pepper

2 teaspoons salt

2 teaspoons olive oil

½ cup beer (use brown ale for more flavor)

½ cup sugar

1. Preheat oven to 350°F.

2. In small bowl, mix pecans, chili powder, red pepper, salt and olive oil. Spread onto foil-lined baking sheet. Toast 5 minutes or until fragrant. Cool on wire rack.

3. Stir together beer and sugar in small saucepan. Heat to 250°F, using candy thermometer to measure temperature. Lower heat.

4. Drizzle sugar mixture over nuts on baking sheet; stir to coat.

5. Let cool. Break up any large pieces and serve in a small dish.

Makes 8 servings

Per Serving: 248.6 calories, 19.6g fat (1.6g saturated, 12.2g monounsaturated, 4.7g polyunsaturated), 0mg cholesterol, 541mg sodium, 18.7g carbohydrate (2.5g dietary fiber), 2.3g protein

Stuffed Poblanos in Walnut Sauce

Spicy Pork Green Chile

Beef & Pork

Beef Tongue in Ranchero Sauce

Shredded Basil Beef Salad

Whether you're preparing everyday fare such as tacos and salads or cooking for an elegant party or dinner, beef and pork dishes are sure to impress and satisfy.

Stuffed Poblanos in Walnut Sauce
Chiles en Nogada

Tip from Chef LaLa

Chiles should be fresh, firm, and shiny. Avoid using dull, soft, or wrinkled chiles; they're are old and will be too soft after they have been seared and skinned. If chiles are fresh, they will be easy to skin and handle when stuffing and cooking.

Remove all of the walnut skins so the sauce stays white and creamy.

½ cup chopped salt pork or bacon
5 garlic cloves, minced
½ pound *each* lean ground beef, pork and veal
¾ cup dried finely chopped apricots
4 cups finely chopped peaches
2 cups peeled and chopped Granny Smith apples
½ ripe plantain or banana, chopped
½ cup raisins
1 cup pitted prunes, finely chopped
2 cups chopped tomatoes
½ teaspoon ground cloves
¼ teaspoon ground nutmeg
2 teaspoons ground cinnamon
4 sprigs fresh thyme
4 bay leaves

1 tablespoon black pepper
1 cup white wine
½ cup dry sherry
2 teaspoons salt
16 medium to large poblano chiles
2 cups shelled walnuts
2 cups raw slivered almonds
4 ounces goat cheese
2 ounces queso cotija
1 slice white bread, crust removed
2 cups half-and-half
1 tablespoon sugar
¼ teaspoon ground cinnamon
¼ cup dry sherry
¼ teaspoon salt
Pomegranate seeds (optional)

1. To make filling, heat large skillet over medium-high heat; add salt pork and brown. Add garlic; cook 1 to 2 minutes. Add beef, pork and veal. Cook, stirring occasionally to break up and separate meat. Stir in apricots, peaches, apples, plantain, raisins, prunes and tomatoes. Lower heat and cook 20 minutes. Add cloves, nutmeg, cinnamon, thyme, bay leaves, pepper, wine, sherry and salt. Simmer 1 hour.

2. Place chiles over high flame and sear until black but still firm. Place chiles in plastic bag 10 minutes; peel. Make a slit on one side about three-fourths the length of the chile. Remove seeds and veins. Place on paper towels; wipe dry. Stuff with filling and refrigerate until ready to serve.

3. Boil walnuts 5 to 8 minutes; drain. Peel skins. Place walnuts, almonds, goat cheese, queso cotija, bread, half-and-half, sugar, cinnamon, sherry and salt in blender or food processor. Purée until smooth. Refrigerate until ready to serve.

4. Place cold chiles on plate topped with walnut sauce. Garnish with pomegranate seeds.

Makes 16 servings

Per Serving: 520 calories, 25g fat (3.8g saturated, 12g monounsaturated, 8g polyunsaturated), 50mg cholesterol, 383mg sodium, 48g carbohydrate (8g dietary fiber), 25g protein

Spicy Pork Green Chile
Chile Verde de Puerco Picante

1 cup canola or vegetable oil

2 pounds pork shoulder, trimmed and cut into medium-sized pieces

1½ pounds tomatillos, peeled

5 fresh serrano chiles, stemmed

2 large garlic cloves

1 ounce canned jalapeño slices, undrained

2 cups water, divided

1 teaspoon cornstarch

1 teaspoon black pepper

1 teaspoon garlic powder

1 tablespoon salt

1. Heat oil in large skillet over medium-high heat. Add pork in batches (do not overcrowd). Brown pork, stirring occasionally. Drain and discard fat. Return pork to skillet.

2. While pork cooks, place tomatillos and chiles in small saucepan; add enough water to cover by 1 inch. Cook over medium heat 15 minutes or until tomatillos are tender. Strain tomatillos and serranos and discard cooking liquid. Place tomatillos in blender with garlic, jalapeño slices and juice and 1 cup water; blend until smooth. Add tomatillo mixture to saucepan with pork. Cook over medium-low heat.

3. Dissolve cornstarch into remaining 1 cup water. Stir cornstarch mixture into pork sauce. Add pepper, garlic powder and salt. Cover and cook 30 minutes, stirring occasionally.

Makes 8 servings

Per Serving: 235 calories, 15g fat (4g saturated, 6.8g monounsaturated, 1.7g polyunsaturated), 60mg cholesterol, 858mg sodium, 9.3g carbohydrate (2.3g dietary fiber), 16.4g protein

Jalisco Style Stew
Birria

Tip from Chef LaLa

For a more flavorful stew, substitute 4 pounds goat meat for bone-in chuck roll.

4 pounds bone-in beef chuck roll

3 garlic cloves, minced

1 teaspoon black pepper

¼ cup apple cider vinegar

1 medium onion, chopped

2½ quarts water

4 bay leaves

2 dried California chiles

2 dried New Mexico chiles

2 dried pasilla chiles

½ medium onion

3 garlic cloves

1 cup water

1 teaspoon minced fresh ginger

4 bay leaves

¼ teaspoon black pepper

8 ounces canned tomato sauce

¼ teaspoon dried oregano

1 large orange, juiced

4 serrano chiles, canned

½ cup juice of canned serrano chiles

1½ tablespoons salt

1 cup chopped onion

1 cup cilantro, finely chopped

Corn tortillas and salsa (optional)

1. Simmer beef, garlic, black pepper, apple cider vinegar, onion, water and bay leaves in large pot 2 hours, covered. Skim any fat from top of pot.

2. Meanwhile, soak chiles 20 minutes in hot water. Remove seeds and tops. Add chiles, onion, garlic, water and ginger to blender and purée until smooth.

3. Preheat oven to 350°F.

4. Remove beef from pot with slotted spoon and place in large roasting or baking pan.

5. Add chile mixture to meat juice in pot. Add bay leaves, black pepper, canned tomato sauce, oregano, orange juice, chiles with juice and salt to pot. Stir to combine.

6. Cover meat halfway with meat-chili juice. (Do not fully cover.) Bake, uncovered, 1 hour.

7. Simmer remaining juice in pot 20 minutes. Reserve.

8. Serve meat with reserved juice. Garnish with onion and cilantro. Serve with corn tortillas and salsa, if desired.

Makes 16 servings

Per Serving: 171 calories, 2.9g fat (.9g saturated, 1.2g monounsaturated, .3g polyunsaturated), 65mg cholesterol, 802mg sodium, 11.3g carbohydrate (2g dietary fiber), 25.5g protein

Beef Tongue in Ranchero Sauce
Lengua Ranchera

Tip from Chef LaLa

This dish can also be made with skirt steak. Cut 3 pounds skirt steak into medium strips and proceed with step 3.

3 pounds beef tongue

2 garlic cloves

½ teaspoon black pepper

¼ cup apple cider vinegar

½ medium onion, quartered

3 bay leaves

Water to cover

¼ cup canola or vegetable oil

½ teaspoon black pepper

½ teaspoon garlic powder

1 tablespoon salt

Ranchero Sauce

2 cups unsalted chicken stock or water

1 tablespoon juice from canned jalapeño peppers

4 bay leaves

¼ teaspoon cumin

8 ounces canned tomato sauce

2 fresh Anaheim chiles, thinly sliced

1 tablespoon canola or vegetable oil

2 tablespoons all-purpose flour

1 green bell pepper, thinly sliced

1 pasilla chile, thinly sliced

½ medium white onion, chopped

4 stalks green onion, chopped

1. Rinse beef and place in 6-quart pot. Add garlic, pepper, vinegar, onion and bay leaves and cover completely with water. Cook 2½ hours or until tender. (Add more water as it evaporates, keeping beef covered.) When beef is tender, remove skin and set aside to cool. Do not remove skin until ready to use.

2. Slice beef in half lengthwise and then into ¼-inch slices.

3. Heat oil in large skillet over medium-high heat. Add sliced meat and sprinkle with pepper, garlic powder and salt. Brown 10 minutes. Cover and cook 5 minutes. Remove from heat; drain fat. Return meat to skillet. Add chicken stock, jalapeño juice, bay leaves, cumin, tomato sauce and Anaheim chiles. Cover and simmer 30 minutes.

4. Heat oil and flour in small skillet over medium heat. Stir constantly until golden brown. Slowly incorporate into meat and juices, stirring constantly. Add bell pepper, pasilla chile and onions. Cover and simmer 10 minutes.

Makes 10 to 12 servings

Per Serving: 339 calories, 25.8g fat (8g saturated, 12g monounsaturated, 2.8g polyunsaturated), 69mg cholesterol, 765mg sodium, 5.3g carbohydrate (1g dietary fiber), 21g protein

Shredded Basil Beef Salad
Ensalada de Res y Albahaca

Tip from Chef LaLa

Soaking the lettuce first keeps it crisp.

Salad

1 pound flank steak

1 quart water

1 bay leaf

½ teaspoon black peppercorns

2 garlic cloves

1 medium head iceberg lettuce, torn into bite-size pieces

4 radishes, thinly sliced

½ medium red onion, thinly sliced

1 medium tomato, cut into 8 slices

½ medium avocado, sliced (optional)

Dressing

1 cup olive oil

½ cup fresh basil leaves

1 teaspoon salt

1 tablespoon red wine vinegar

¼ teaspoon black pepper

2 cloves garlic

1. Cook flank steak, water, bay leaf, peppercorns and garlic over medium heat 1½ to 2 hours, covered. Remove steak from liquid and shred.

2. Soak lettuce in ice cold water 15 minutes. Drain.

3. Make dressing by adding olive oil, basil, salt, vinegar, pepper and garlic to blender or food processor and purée until smooth.

4. Place lettuce, meat, radishes, onion and tomato in large bowl. Toss to combine. Add dressing. Garnish with avocado slices.

Makes 16 servings

Per Serving (salad): 189 calories, 17g fat (3.2g saturated, 11.8g monounsaturated, 1.4g polyunsaturated), 14mg cholesterol, 160mg sodium, 2.5g carbohydrate (1.1g dietary fiber), 6.2g protein

Per Serving (dressing): 122 calories, 13.5g fat (.5g saturated, 10g monounsaturated, 1.1g polyunsaturated), 0mg cholesterol, 134mg sodium, .3g carbohydrate (0g dietary fiber), 2g protein

Mexican-Style Sausage
Chorizo Mexicano

1 pound extra-lean ground pork

2 tablespoons apple cider vinegar

1½ tablespoons water

1 tablespoon red chili powder

2 tablespoons ancho chile powder

1 tablespoon dried red pepper, crushed

4 cloves garlic, minced

1 tablespoon dried oregano

1 teaspoon cumin seeds, crushed

1 teaspoon sugar

½ teaspoon black pepper

2½ teaspoons salt

Warm corn tortillas

Place all ingredients except tortillas in blender or food processor and pulse until incorporated. Stuff in casings, if desired. Serve with tortillas.

Makes 4 servings

Per Serving: 70 calories, 4g fat (1.2g saturated, 1.6g monounsaturated, .4g polyunsaturated), 19mg cholesterol, 487mg sodium, 2.9g carbohydrate (1g dietary fiber), 6g protein

Tip from Chef LaLa

Chorizo is a sausage. The word "sausage" is derived from the Latin word "salsicia (something salted). Sausage is made in Spain, Portugal, Mexico and other Latin countries.

Picadillo Tacos
Tacos de Picadillo

8 ounces lean ground beef

2 ounces tomato sauce

¼ cup chopped onion

½ teaspoon chili powder

½ teaspoon garlic salt

¼ teaspoon black pepper

6 (6- to 7-inch) corn tortillas, warmed

½ cup low-fat Cheddar cheese, shredded

1 cup shredded lettuce

1 small tomato, chopped

Salsa (optional)

1. Heat medium skillet over medium-high heat. Add beef, brown 3 to 4 minutes, breaking up meat with spatula. Add tomato sauce, onions, chili powder, garlic salt and pepper. Stir to combine. Lower heat, cover and cook 3 to 5 minutes.

2. Heat tortillas on griddle until pliable. Fill with meat, cheese, lettuce and tomato and fold in half. Serve with salsa, if desired.

Makes 6 tacos

Per Serving (1 taco): 186.7 calories, 8.7g fat (3.5g saturated, 3.5g monounsaturated, 0g polyunsaturated), 27mg cholesterol, 207mg sodium, 14.2g carbohydrate (2g dietary fiber), 11.2g protein

Yucatán Achiote Pork Tacos
Tacos de Cochinita Pibil Estilo Yucatán

Tip from Chef LaLa

In Yucatán, the entire pig is marinated in achiote mixture, wrapped in banana leaves and slowly cooked underground. The 2 meats (shoulder and ribs), vary in texture and flavor. Bacon helps maintain moisture and give it a smoky flavor.

8 garlic cloves, sliced

2 tablespoons salt

⅓ cup white vinegar

½ teaspoon ground allspice

1 tablespoon minced fresh oregano

3½ ounces achiote paste

⅓ cup lime juice

⅓ cup orange juice

4 pounds pork shoulder

1½ to 2 pounds baby back ribs

1 medium white onion, sliced

8 slices bacon

5 medium red onions, thinly sliced

6 limes, juiced

3 oranges, juiced

36 corn tortillas

Grandma's Salsa (see page 35)

1. Combine garlic, salt, vinegar, allspice, oregano, achiote paste, lime and orange juices in large bowl.

2. Preheat oven to 200°F. Place pork shoulder and ribs in roasting pan or Dutch oven; cover with achiote mixture. Lay onion over meat and cover with bacon slices. Cover pan tightly with aluminum foil and bake 5 hours.

3. Meanwhile, combine onion with lime and orange juices in small bowl and let marinate in refrigerator until ready to use.

4. Remove pan from oven; skim off fat. Heat tortillas on griddle until soft and pliable. Fill with meat. Serve with marinated onions and salsa.

Makes 36 to 40 tacos

Per Serving (1 taco): 223 calories, 13.4g fat (4.6g saturated, 5.9g monounsaturated, 1.5g polyunsaturated), 510mg cholesterol, 502mg sodium, 12.5g carbohydrate (1.4g dietary fiber), 13.1g protein

Tequila Onion Steak
Filete con Cebolla en Tequila

1 medium onion,
   sliced into rings

¼ cup tequila

1 teaspoon salt

1 tablespoon fresh cilantro

3 garlic cloves

½ teaspoon black pepper

2 dried chipotle peppers

1 tomato

2 tablespoons olive oil

2 pounds top sirloin or
   New York strip steak

1 teaspoon olive oil

Salt to taste

1. Place onions, tequila and salt in resealable food storage bag. Marinate in refrigerator 2 hours.

2. Place cilantro and garlic in blender with pepper, chipotle peppers, tomato and olive oil; purée until smooth. Pour mixture over meat. Marinate 2 hours.

3. Preheat grill to high. Remove steak from marinade; shake off excess. Lightly coat both sides of each steak with oil. Sprinkle with salt. Sear steaks 4 to 5 minutes on each side or to desired doneness. When done, transfer to warmed platter and allow to rest 2 to 3 minutes before slicing. Top with marinated tequila onions.

Makes 8 servings

Per Serving: 587 calories, 39.4g fat (14g saturated, 18.8g monounsaturated, 2g polyunsaturated), 144mg cholesterol, 790mg sodium, 6.2g carbohydrate (1.3g dietary fiber), 42.6g protein

Pork and Plum Kabobs
Alambre de Puerco y Ciruela

2 dried chiles negros

2 dried ancho or pasillo chiles

6 tomatillos, peeled

3 garlic cloves

½ medium onion

¼ cup almonds, slivered, peeled

1 cup water

3 black plums, ripe but firm, pitted and diced

2 tablespoons sugar

1 teaspoon salt

1 pound pork tenderloin, cut into large pieces

¼ teaspoon garlic powder

½ teaspoon salt

½ teaspoon black pepper

1 tablespoon canola or vegetable oil

3 black plums, ripe but firm, cut into 6 wedges each

8 wooden skewers

1. Toast chiles negros and anchos on skillet or griddle. (Be careful not to burn them or they will get bitter.) Transfer to medium bowl; cover with hot water and soak until soft, about 30 minutes.

2. Char tomatillos, garlic and onion in skillet.

3. Place chiles, almonds, tomatillos, water and plums in blender and purée until smooth. Transfer to large skillet; add sugar and salt. Simmer 20 minutes, covered.

4. Sprinkle pork tenderloin with garlic powder, salt and pepper. Heat oil in medium skillet over medium-high heat. Add meat, browning on all sides, about 1 minute per side. Remove and set aside.

5. Alternately thread pork and plum wedges onto skewers. Simmer skewers in chile sauce 5 to 10 minutes. Serve with extra side of sauce for dipping.

Makes 8 servings

Per Serving (1 skewer): 393 calories, 27g fat (9.2g saturated, 12.4g monounsaturated, 2.8g polyunsaturated), 82mg cholesterol, 505mg sodium, 16.7g carbohydrate (2.5g dietary fiber), 22g protein

Beef Red Chile
Chile Colorado de Res

Tip from Chef LaLa

Beef Red Chile is a family favorite. This is my grandfather Donato's recipe.

¼ cup canola or vegetable oil

4 pounds chuck roll beef, trimmed and cut into medium-sized pieces

3 garlic cloves, minced

1 tablespoon soy sauce

1 tablespoon black pepper

2 dried New Mexico chiles

2 dried California chiles

2 dried guajillo chiles

3 cups hot water

1 garlic clove, peeled

¼ medium onion, quartered

1 cup water

½ teaspoon salt

¼ cup canola or vegetable oil

2 tablespoons all-purpose flour

⅛ teaspoon ground cinnamon

¼ teaspoon dried oregano

½ tablespoon salt

1. Heat oil in large skillet over medium-high heat. Add beef, garlic, soy sauce and black pepper. Cover and cook 30 minutes. Uncover and cook until juices evaporate, about 15 minutes.

2. Meanwhile, soak chiles in 3 cups hot water 20 minutes. Remove seeds and tops; drain and discard water. Place chiles and garlic in blender with onion, 1 cup water and salt; purée until smooth. Pour mixture over meat.

3. Heat oil and flour in small skillet over medium heat. Stir constantly until golden brown. Slowly incorporate into meat and sauce while stirring. Add cinnamon, oregano and salt. Lower heat; simmer 30 minutes or until meat is tender.

Makes 16 servings

Per Serving: 325 calories, 24.7g fat (7.8g saturated, 11.6g monounsaturated, 2.5g polyunsaturated), 66mg cholesterol, 188mg sodium, 6.7g carbohydrate (1g dietary fiber), 19.3g protein

Pork Chops 'n' Fruit Salsa
Chuletas con Fruta

Tip from Chef LaLa

Today, pork is an important part of a healthy diet. Since the 1980s, the fat content of pork has been dramatically reduced. Pork tenderloin is now 42% lower in fat. This improvement is due to better breeding and feeding practices and more thorough fat trimming by processors and stores.

This salsa is great as a dip or can be served with grilled fish, chicken, or pork.

¼ teaspoon salt

¼ teaspoon black pepper

Dash garlic powder

½ teaspoon olive oil

6 ounces cola

1 pound thick-cut pork chops, fat trimmed

½ teaspoon canola or vegetable oil

Fruit Salsa (recipe follows)

1. Combine salt, pepper, garlic powder, olive oil and cola in large bowl. Place pork chop in mixture. Cover and refrigerate 45 minutes.

2. Preheat oven to 325°F. Heat oil in large skillet. Add pork; sear both sides 5 minutes each or until golden brown. Finish cooking in oven 15 to 20 minutes. Serve with salsa.

Makes 3 servings

Per Serving: 218 calories, 12.8g fat (4.4g saturated, 8.4g unsaturated), 68mg cholesterol, 51mg sodium, 0g carbohydrate (0g dietary fiber), 24g protein

Fruit Salsa
Salsa de Frutas

½ cup peeled and finely chopped pineapple

1 cup finely chopped peaches

6 strawberries, sliced ⅛-inch thick

½ jalapeño pepper, finely chopped

2 tablespoons chopped fresh cilantro

¼ cup finely chopped red onion

2 green onions (green part only), chopped

½ teaspoon salt

3 tablespoons water

½ orange, juiced

Combine all ingredients in large bowl. Chill 2 hours and serve.

Makes 12 servings

Per Serving: 50 calories, .4g fat (0g saturated, .1g unsaturated), 0mg cholesterol, 92mg sodium, 12.6g carbohydrate (2.6g dietary fiber), 1.1g protein

Spicy Pork Red Chile
Chile Colorado de Puerco Picante

1 cup canola or vegetable oil

2 pounds pork shoulder, trimmed and cut into medium chunks

5 dried Japanese chiles, stems removed

3 dried árbol chiles, stems removed

1 can (11 ounces) roasted, peeled canned tomatoes

2 large garlic cloves

1 ounce canned jalapeño pepper slices, undrained

2 cups water, divided

1 teaspoon cornstarch

1 teaspoon black pepper

1 teaspoon garlic powder

1 tablespoon salt

1. Heat oil in large skillet over medium-high heat. Add pork in batches (do not overcrowd). Brown pork; drain. Return pork to skillet.

2. While pork cooks, place chiles in small skillet and toast.

3. Place tomatoes and toasted chiles in blender with garlic, jalapeño slices and juice and 1 cup water; purée until smooth. Add tomato mixture to skillet with pork. Cook over medium-low heat.

4. Dissolve cornstarch in 1 cup water. Stir cornstarch mixture into pork sauce. Add pepper, garlic powder and salt. Cover and cook 30 minutes, stirring occasionally.

Makes 8 servings

Per Serving: 216 calories, 14g fat (4g saturated, 6.9g monounsaturated, 1.7g polyunsaturated), 60mg cholesterol, 921mg sodium, 6g carbohydrate (1g dietary fiber), 15.9g protein

Tip from Chef LaLa

When toasting chiles, open all windows in your home — these spicy chiles will make you cough.

Use this recipe when making Divorced Eggs (see page 15).

Rachel's Enchiladas
Enchiladas Raquel

Tip from Chef LaLa

As the "bread" of Mexico, corn tortillas are much more nutritious than plain corn because of nixtamalization, the process of making corn into masa (classic corn dough). This process increases the protein value of corn by releasing bound niacin.

1 pound extra-lean ground beef

¾ pound potatoes, peeled and quartered

⅓ cup water

1 teaspoon salt, divided

6 ounces canned tomatoes, undrained

2 garlic cloves, peeled

½ onion, quartered

2 serrano chiles

4 cups beef or vegetable broth

1 tostada (see page 12)

¼ teaspoon black pepper

Dash cumin

14 corn tortillas

12 ounces cotija cheese

1. Place ground beef, potatoes and water in large pot. Cover and cook over medium-low heat 20 minutes or until potatoes are tender. Drain and reserve broth.

2. Mash meat and potatoes together with potato masher. Mix in ½ teaspoon salt.

3. Place reserved broth in blender with canned tomatoes, ½ teaspoon salt, garlic, onion, chiles, broth, tostada, pepper and cumin. Purée until smooth; transfer to saucepan. Simmer 20 minutes.

4. Preheat oven to 375°F. Dip tortilla into saucepan; carefully and quickly transfer onto baking pan. Spoon ¼ cup filling down center of tortilla. Roll up tortilla; place seam-side down in baking pan. Arrange rolls closely to each other. Repeat with each tortilla. Cover with sauce.

5. Bake 5 to 7 minutes. Serve immediately. Sprinkle with crumbled cotija.

Makes 14 enchiladas (Sauce makes 4½ cups)

Per Serving: 180 calories, 7.9g fat (2.9g saturated, 5g unsaturated), 300mg cholesterol, 279mg sodium, 19g carbohydrate (2.2g dietary fiber), 8.5g protein

Charbroiled Skirt Steak
Carne Asada

1 cup water

3 tablespoons low-sodium
soy sauce

½ cup onion, sliced

4 tablespoons fresh cilantro,
torn into pieces

1 garlic clove, peeled and sliced

1 teaspoon extra-virgin olive oil

1 teaspoon unsalted meat
tenderizer

¼ teaspoon black pepper

½ orange

3 pounds skirt steak, fat trimmed
and butterflied

Tip from Chef LaLa

To find the leanest cuts of beef, look for the word "round" or "loin" in the name.

1. Combine water, soy sauce, onion, cilantro, garlic, olive oil, meat tenderizer, pepper and orange in large bowl. Add meat; cover both sides with marinade. Cover and refrigerate 4 hours.

2. Heat grill to medium heat. Place meat on grill. Turn steak once during cooking. Cook to desired doneness (5 minutes on each side for medium-rare).

Makes 12 servings

Per Serving: 212 calories, 12.3g fat (5.1g saturated, 7.2g unsaturated), 580mg cholesterol, 237mg sodium, 1g carbohydrate (4g dietary fiber), 22.4g protein

Mole Poblano

Chicken Tamales

Poultry

Citrus-Garlic Charbroiled Chicken

Green Chicken Enchiladas

Poultry is a mainstay in Mexican cuisine. Widely available, economical, and versatile, poultry can be found on every menu and in every kitchen. It's a key ingredient in everything from classic tamales to spicy, savory mole.

Mole Poblano
Mole Poblano

12 cups water
1 (3½- to 4-pound) skinless, bone-in chicken, cut into pieces
1 chopped medium onion
1 chopped celery stalk
2 sliced carrots
1 teaspoon chicken bouillon

Mole Sauce

8 dried ancho chiles
8 dried pasilla chiles
1 dried chipotle chile
4 cups water
2 medium tomatoes
4 tomatillos, peeled
14 garlic cloves
2 medium onions
½ cup canola or vegetable oil
1 corn tortilla
½ cup almonds, peeled
½ cup unsalted peanuts
½ cup sesame seeds, toasted
1 ripe plantain or banana
½ cup pitted prunes
½ cup seedless raisins
4 avocado leaves (optional)
½ teaspoon ground anise
5 black peppercorns
4 cloves
1 cinnamon stick
½ teaspoon cumin seeds
1 medium French roll, chopped into bite-size pieces
2 tablespoons sugar
1 ounce Mexican chocolate
½ teaspoon salt
½ cup sesame seeds (optional)

1. Combine water, chicken, onion, celery, carrots and bouillon in large pot and cook over medium-low heat 1 hour. Remove chicken pieces and set aside; reserve broth.

2. Toast chiles in small skillet. Transfer to medium bowl with hot water and soak until soft, 30 minutes. Meanwhile, char tomatoes, tomatillos, garlic and onion in a large skillet. Set aside.

3. Heat canola oil in large pot. Fry corn tortilla. Set aside. Add almonds, peanuts and sesame seeds. Cook 2 minutes. Add plantain, prunes, raisins, avocado leaves, if desired, anise, peppercorns, cloves, cinnamon, cumin and bread. Cook 10 minutes. Add plantain mixutre to blender or food processor with 1 cup reserved broth; purée until smooth. Return to pot. Drain toasted chiles and purée with additional 1 cup reserved chicken broth until smooth. Add to pot with plantain mixture. Add tomatillo mixture to blender with reserved tortilla and ½ cup broth; purée until smooth. Add to pot with plantain and chile mixtures. Add sugar and chocolate. Cover; cook over low heat 2 hours, stirring occasionally. Add salt.

4. Just before serving, return chicken pieces to pot and boil 10 minutes. Serve on platter. Garnish with sesame seeds.

Makes 8 (2-piece) servings

Per Serving: 772 calories, 42g fat (7g saturated, 20g monounsaturated, 11.9g polyunsaturated), 124mg cholesterol, 601mg sodium, 52.7g carbohydrate (9.4g dietary fiber), 51.4g protein

Chicken Tamales
Tamales de Pollo

8 ounces corn husks

1 (3½- to 4-pound) whole chicken

1 onion, halved

2 cloves garlic

3 quarts water

1 tablespoon dried oregano

2 tablespoons canola or vegetable oil

1 clove garlic, minced

1 medium potato, thickly sliced

1 large carrot, thickly sliced

1 cup green peas

4 ounces tomato paste

½ tablespoon salt

½ tablespoon black pepper

½ tablespoon garlic powder

1 cup canned Anaheim chiles, roasted

3 pounds prepared tamale masa

1. Soak husks in large bowl filled with warm water 2 hours. Carefully separate when softened and lay on a towel to dry.

2. Cook chicken, half of onion, garlic, water and oregano in large pot, covered, over medium heat 30 minutes. Remove chicken; cool. Shred into medium-sized pieces. Reserve broth.

3. Heat oil in large skillet over medium heat. Cook and stir onions and garlic 3 minutes. Add potato and carrot; cook 4 minutes. Add shredded chicken, peas, tomato paste, reserved broth, salt, pepper and garlic powder. Cover; simmer 10 minutes. Add chiles; stir to combine. Remove from heat. Uncover and cool.

4. Spoon prepared masa into center of husk. Add small amount of filling in center and bring sides together, folding to enclose filling. Twist ends of tamale and secure with small strip of husk.

5. Place in steamer. Cover with tight-fitting lid and steam 1 hour, adding water as needed. Tamales are ready when masa pulls away from husks.

Makes 3 dozen tamales

Per Serving (1 tamale): 250 calories, 9.6g fat (1.2g saturated, 4.7g monounsaturated, 3g polyunsaturated), 21mg cholesterol, 179mg sodium, 31.7g carbohydrate (5.6g dietary fiber), 10g protein

Citrus-Garlic Charbroiled Chicken
Pollo Cítrico Asado

3 garlic cloves

1 orange, peeled and quartered

1 lime, peeled and quartered

1 cup chopped fresh pineapple

2 cups water

1 teaspoon yellow food coloring

2 tablespoons salt

1 tablespoon garlic powder

1 tablespoon black pepper

2 (3½- to 4-pound) whole chickens

1. Place garlic and orange in blender or food processor with lime, pineapple, water, food coloring, salt, garlic powder and pepper; blend until smooth.

2. Cut chickens in half. Spread blended mixture over chicken in shallow dish and marinate in refrigerator 3 hours.

3. Grill chickens over low heat until done and juices run clear, about 1 to 1½ hours. Cut chickens into 8 pieces. Serve with rice, beans, warm tortillas and salsa.

Makes 16 pieces

Per Serving (2 pieces): 242 calories, 9g fat (2.4g saturated, 3.3g monounsaturated, 2.2g polyunsaturated), 93mg cholesterol, 890mg sodium, 8.7g carbohydrate (1.2g dietary fiber), 30g protein

Green Chicken Enchiladas
Enchiladas Suizas

1 pound tomatillos, peeled

2 garlic cloves

¼ small onion

¼ cup fresh cilantro

½ cup chicken broth

2 tablespoons canola or vegetable oil

1 tablespoon all-purpose flour

1½ pounds boneless, skinless cooked chicken breasts, shredded

6 ounces cotija cheese or feta cheese

1 cup canola or vegetable oil

20 corn tortillas

6 ounces queso fresco or Monterey Jack cheese

½ cup shredded cilantro (optional)

1. Make enchilada sauce by placing tomatillos in small saucepan; add enough water to cover by 1 inch. Cook over medium heat 15 minutes or until tomatillos are tender. Strain tomatillos and discard cooking liquid. Place tomatillos in blender or food processor with garlic, onion, cilantro and broth; purée until smooth. Heat 2 tablespoons oil in medium skillet over medium heat. Add flour and stir until brown. Add enchilada sauce to skillet. Stir to combine. Lower heat and cook 15 minutes, stirring occasionally.

2. In mixing bowl, combine chicken, cotija cheese and 3 tablespoons enchilada sauce. Set aside.

3. Heat 1 cup oil in medium skillet. Dip each tortilla, 1 at a time, in oil until soft (about 10 seconds). Place tortillas on baking pan. Spoon one-fourth chicken and cheese mixture into tortilla. Roll up tortilla; place seam-side down into skillet.

4. Cover enchiladas with warm sauce. Top with queso fresco. Heat over medium heat 5 minutes or until warm. Garnish with cilantro. Serve immediately.

Makes 20 enchiladas

Per Serving (1 enchilada): 164 calories, 8g fat (2.4g saturated, 2.8g monounsaturated, 1.6g polyunsaturated), 19mg cholesterol, 200mg sodium, 14g carbohydrate (1.8g dietary fiber), 8.9g protein

Picante Cornish Hens
Codornices Picantes

Tip from Chef LaLa

If you don't like spicy food, replace red pepper with paprika.

Cornish game hens look just like miniature chickens, and the flavor is the same. They weigh from 1 to 2 pounds, but the standard is about 1½ pounds.

2 fresh or thawed frozen Cornish hens (1½ pounds each)

3 tablespoons fresh lemon juice

3 cloves garlic, minced

2 tablespoons olive oil

¼ cup orange marmalade

2 teaspoons ground mustard

1 teaspoon ground red pepper

1 teaspoon paprika

2 teaspoons ground cinnamon

½ teaspoon ground cloves

2 tablespoons chicken bouillon

1. Remove giblets from cavities of hens; reserve for another use or discard. Split hens in half on cutting board with sharp knife or poultry shears, cutting through breastbones and backbones. Rinse with cold water; pat dry with paper towels. Place hens in large resealable food storage bag.

2. Combine lemon juice and garlic in small bowl; pour over hens. Seal bag; turn to coat. Marinate in refrigerator 1 hour.

3. Meanwhile, prepare grill for direct cooking.

4. Drain hens, discarding marinade. Brush with oil. Place hens, skin-side up, on grid. Grill hens, covered, over medium-low coals 25 minutes, turning once.

5. Meanwhile, combine marmalade, mustard, red pepper, paprika, cinnamon, cloves and chicken bouillon in small bowl. Brush half marmalade mixture evenly over hens, cook 10 minutes. Brush with remaining mixture. Grill, covered, 5 to 10 minutes or until juices run clear. Serve immediately.

Makes 4 servings

Per Serving (½ hen): 812 calories, 46.5g fat (11.9g saturated, 20g monounsaturated, 9g polyunsaturated), 248mg cholesterol, 959mg sodium, 19g carbohydrate (2.7g dietary fiber), 78g protein

Grilled Chicken Tostada
Tostada de Pollo a la Parilla

1 pound boneless, skinless chicken breast halves

½ teaspoon red pepper flakes

½ teaspoon garlic powder

½ teaspoon dried oregano

3 teaspoons olive oil, divided

1 teaspoon salt

6 green onion stalks

1 cup canned refried beans (or see recipe on page 70)

6 (6- to 7-inch) wheat or flour tortillas

2 cups chopped romaine lettuce

6 ounces queso cotija or shredded Monterey Jack cheese

1 medium avocado, chopped

1 medium tomato, seeded and chopped

¼ cup chopped fresh cilantro (optional)

½ cup crema fresca or sour cream (optional)

1. Place chicken in single layer in shallow glass dish; sprinkle with pepper flakes, garlic powder, oregano, 1 teaspoon olive oil and salt. Stir to combine. Cover; marinate in refrigerator at least 2 hours or up to 8 hours, stirring mixture occasionally.

2. Prepare grill for direct cooking.

3. Drain chicken and reserve marinade. Brush green onions with remaining 2 teaspoons oil. Place chicken and green onions on grid. Grill, covered, over medium-high heat 5 minutes. Brush tops of chicken with half of reserved marinade; turn and brush with remaining marinade. Turn onions. Continue to grill, covered, 5 minutes or until chicken is no longer pink in center and onions are tender. (If onions brown too quickly, remove before chicken is done.)

4. Meanwhile, heat refried beans in small skillet until hot.

5. Place tortillas in single layer on grid. Grill, uncovered, 1 to 2 minutes per side or until golden brown. (If tortillas puff up, pierce with tip of knife or flatten by pressing with spatula.)

6. Transfer chicken and onions to cutting board. Slice chicken crosswise into ½-inch strips. Cut onions crosswise into 1-inch-long pieces. Spread tortillas with bean mixture; top with lettuce, chicken, onions, cheese, avocado and tomato. Sprinkle with cilantro and serve with sour cream.

Makes 6 servings

Per 1-cup Serving: 414 calories, 19.8g fat (7.8g saturated, 75.2g monounsaturated, 2.5g polyunsaturated), 55mg cholesterol, 972mg sodium, 32g carbohydrate (13.1g dietary fiber), 28g protein

Empanaditas
Empanaditas

Tip from Chef LaLa

If you don't own a food processor, you can combine all ingredients in a bowl and knead by hand.

It's important to lightly dust the surface and rolling pin or the dough will get too dry.

Dough

- ¾ cup flour
- ¾ cup masa harina
- ¾ teaspoon salt
- ½ cup ice water
- 3 tablespoons butter, cut into small pieces
- 12 sheets waxed paper cut into 4 × 4-inch pieces
- Flour (for dusting)

Filling

- ½ cup chopped zucchini
- 1 pasilla chile, roasted, chopped
- ½ cup cooked chicken, shredded
- ½ cup queso fresco, crumbled
- 1 tablespoon green onion, minced
- Salt to taste
- 2 egg yolks
- 2 teaspoons water

1. Place flour, masa harina and salt in blender or food processor; pulse. Incorporate water while pulsing. Add butter and continue to pulse to form a dough ball.

2. Remove dough from food processor and knead. Divide dough into 12 equal balls; cover with damp towel to keep dough from drying. Lightly sprinkle a flat, clean surface with flour. Sprinkle rolling pin with flour. Roll out each dough ball into 3-inch circles. Stack circles on top of each other, separating each circle with a sheet of waxed paper. Refrigerate 1 hour.

3. Preheat oven to 400°F. Combine zucchini, chile, chicken, queso fresco and onion in medium bowl. Salt to taste.

4. Wisk together egg yolks and water in small bowl. Remove dough from refrigerator. Place about 1 teaspoon filling on each circle. Fold over dough to make half moons. Brush inside corner with egg mixture to seal. Seal edges by pressing down with fork; brush with egg mixture. Place on ungreased baking sheets. Bake 20 minutes or until golden brown.

Makes 12 empanaditas

Per Serving (1 empanadita): 105 calories, 4.1g fat (2.2g saturated, 1.2g monounsaturated, .4g polyunsaturated), 15mg cholesterol, 175mg sodium, 13.1g carbohydrate (1g dietary fiber), 4.2g protein

Cheesy Chicken Flautas
Flautas de pollo con Queso Chicloso

Tip from Chef LaLa

To bake instead of fry, heat tortillas on a griddle until pliable. Spoon 2 tablespoons of the shredded chicken mixture on one end of each tortilla and roll tightly to resemble a cigar. Place seam-side down on a baking sheet. Repeat with remaining ingredients. Bake filled flautas 15 minutes or until golden and crisp. Serve with salsa.

4 cups water

1 pound boneless, skinless chicken breast halves

Salt to taste

6 ounces shredded low-fat Colby, Monterey Jack, or Cheddar cheese

½ teaspoon salt

¼ teaspoon black pepper

16 soft corn tortillas

1 cup canola or vegetable oil

2 cups Grandma's Salsa (see page 35)

1. Add water to large saucepan and bring to boil over high heat. Add chicken and salt. Bring just to boil; reduce heat. Cover and simmer 15 minutes or until chicken is no longer pink in center. Remove chicken from pan, discard cooking water; shred chicken into thin strips. In medium bowl combine chicken, cheese, salt and pepper.

2. Heat tortillas on griddle until pliable. Place thin strip of filling lenthwise on tortillas and roll tightly in flute shape ("flauta" in Spanish). Secure with wooden toothpicks.

3. Fill large skillet with ½ inch oil and heat over medium-high. Fry flautas 3 to 4 minutes or until crisp and golden brown on all sides. Remove from pan and place on plate covered with paper towels. Wipe off excess oil and remove toothpicks. Serve with salsa.

Makes 16 flautas

Per Serving (1 fried flauta with salsa): 160 calories, 6.5g fat (1.3g saturated, 2.9g monounsaturated, 1.7g polyunsaturated), 19mg cholesterol, 217g sodium, 12.5g carbohydrate (1.5g dietary fiber), 10.7g protein

Festive Cups
Tasitas Festivas

1 tablespoon olive oil

¼ cup finely chopped onion

½ pound ground turkey
or ground beef

1 garlic clove, minced

½ teaspoon dried oregano

½ teaspoon chili powder

¼ teaspoon ground cumin

¼ teaspoon chicken bouillon

1 tablespoon finely chopped mint

1 serrano chile, seeded and
minced (optional)

1 can (11½ ounces) refrigerated
corn breadstick dough

1 medium tomato, seeded and
chopped (optional)

2 green onion stalks, sliced
(optional)

1. Heat oil in large skillet over medium heat. Add onion; cook until tender. Add turkey; cook until turkey is no longer pink, stirring occasionally. Stir in garlic, oregano, chili powder, cumin, chicken bouillon, mint and chile, if desired. Set aside.

2. Preheat oven to 375°F. Lightly grease 36 mini (1¾-inch) muffin cups. Remove dough from container but do not unroll. Separate dough into 8 pieces at perforations. Divide each piece into 3 pieces; roll or pat each piece into 3-inch circle. Press circles into prepared muffin cups.

3. Fill each cup with 1½ to 2 teaspoons turkey mixture. Bake 10 minutes. Garnish with tomato and green onion.

Makes 24 cups

Per 1-cup Serving (with turkey): 67 calories, 3.1g fat (.7g saturated, 1.7g monounsaturated, 5g polyunsaturated), 5mg cholesterol, 165g sodium, 7.5g carbohydrate (.5g dietary fiber), 2.7g protein

Griddle Chicken with Cilantro Salsa
Pollo a la Plancha con Salsa de Cilantro

Marinade

2 New Mexico chiles, toasted

2 cups hot water

2 garlic cloves, minced

¼ medium onion, chopped

1 cup water

½ teaspoon salt

½ teaspoon black pepper

1 tablespoon olive oil

1 pound boneless, skinless chicken breasts

Salsa

1 cup finely chopped cilantro

1 habañero chile, minced

½ medium onion, minced

½ cup olive oil

½ teaspoon salt

1. Soak chiles 20 minutes in hot water. Remove seeds and tops. Drain water and discard. Place chiles in blender with garlic, onion, water, salt, black pepper and olive oil; purée until smooth. In resealable food storage bag, add chicken and pour in chile mixture. Marinate in refrigerator 3 hours.

2. Meanwhile, combine cilantro, habañero, onion, olive oil and salt. Refrigerate at least 3 hours.

3. Remove chicken from bag and drain excess liquid. Heat griddle to medium-high heat. Place chicken on griddle. Place a weight on top of chicken breast (small skillet works well). Do not cover. Cook 3 to 5 minutes on each side or until juices run clear. Transfer chicken to serving plate and top with salsa.

Makes 4 servings

Per Serving (with cilantro salsa): 456 calories, 32.8g fat (4.6g saturated, 22.8g monounsaturated, 3.1g polyunsaturated), 66mg cholesterol, 736mg sodium, 12.6g carbohydrate (2.4g dietary fiber), 29.8g protein

Per Serving (without cilantro salsa): 214 calories, 5.8g fat (1.0g saturated, 2.9g monounsaturated, .8g polyunsaturated), 66mg cholesterol, 401mg sodium, 11.9g carbohydrate (2.1g dietary fiber), 29.6g protein

Puerto Nuevo Lobster

Fish Tacos with Yogurt Sauce

Seafood & Vegetarian

Fillets with Mole Verde

Tequila Garlic Shrimp

Cross oceans and travel the world without leaving your kitchen with these recipes—a hot, fresh fish off the grill; a melt-in-your-mouth buttery lobster tail; a tangy, colorful bean salad, and much more.

Puerto Nuevo Lobster
Langosta Puerto Nuevo

½ cup butter, clarified

4 fresh or frozen lobster tails, thawed (about 5 ounces each)

Tasty Butters (recipe follows)

Beans, rice and flour tortillas (optional)

1. Prepare grill for direct cooking. Prepare desired Tasty Butters.

2. Rinse lobster tails in cold water. Butterfly tails by cutting lengthwise through centers of hard top shells and meat. Cut to, but not through, bottoms of shells. Press shell halves of tails apart with fingers. Brush lobster meat with clarified butter.

3. Place tails on grid, meat side down. Grill, uncovered, over medium-high heat 4 minutes. Turn tails meat side up. Brush with clarified butter. Cook 4 to 5 minutes or until lobster meat turns opaque.

4. Heat Tasty Butter mixtures, stirring occasionally. Serve lobster with Tasty Butters for dipping, beans, rice and flour tortillas, if desired.

Makes 4 servings

Per Serving: 455 calories, 25g fat (14.7g saturated, 7.3g monounsaturated, 1.3g polyunsaturated), 331mg cholesterol, 1070mg sodium, 1.4g carbohydrate (0g dietary fiber), 53g protein

Tasty Butters
Mantequillas Sabrosas

Hot & Spicy Butter

⅓ cup butter, melted

1 tablespoon finely chopped onion

2 to 3 teaspoons hot pepper sauce

1 teaspoon dried thyme

¼ teaspoon ground allspice

Green Onion Butter

⅓ cup butter, melted

1 tablespoon finely chopped green onion top

1 tablespoon lemon juice

1 teaspoon freshly grated lemon peel

¼ teaspoon black pepper

Chili-Mustard Butter

⅓ cup butter, melted

1 tablespoon finely chopped onion

1 tablespoon Dijon mustard

1 teaspoon chili powder

For each butter sauce, combine ingredients in small bowl.

Fish Tacos with Yogurt Sauce
Tacos de Pescado

Tip from Chef LaLa

Serve with Grandma's Salsa (see page 35).

Sauce

½ cup plain yogurt

1 tablespoon low-fat mayonnaise

3 tablespoons light sour cream

¼ teaspoon ground red pepper

½ lime, juiced

¼ cup chopped fresh cilantro

½ teaspoon salt

¼ teaspoon black pepper

½ cup cornstarch

½ teaspoon salt

¼ teaspoon black pepper

1½ pounds tilapia fillets

2 tablespoons canola or vegetable oil

12 corn tortillas

3 cups finely shredded red and green cabbage

1¼ cups finely chopped tomatoes

1. Mix yogurt, mayonnaise, sour cream, red pepper, lime juice, cilantro, salt and pepper in a small bowl. Set aside.

2. Mix cornstarch, salt and pepper on large, flat plate. Place fish in cornstarch mixture; turn to coat both sides with cornstarch mixture.

3. Heat oil in large skillet. Shake excess cornstarch off fish; place fish in pan. Cook fish 3 minutes; turn fish and cook 3 more minutes. Remove from pan and place on paper towels to drain excess oil.

4. Place tortillas on grill or griddle over medium heat 10 seconds on each side, or until beginning to bubble and brown lightly. Fill tortillas with fish. Top with yogurt sauce, cabbage and tomatoes.

Makes 12 tacos

Per Serving (1 taco): 193 calories, 5.6g fat (.9g saturated, 2.5g monounsaturated, 1.6g polyunsaturated), 26mg cholesterol, 383mg sodium, 21.4g carbohydrate (1.4g dietary fiber), 13.8g protein

Catfish with Cherry Salsa
Siluro (Bagre) con Salsa de la Cereza

Cherry Salsa

1 cup fresh sweet cherries, halved and pitted

¼ cup minced red onion

1 medium jalapeño pepper, cored, seeded and minced*

1 tablespoon lime juice

⅓ cup orange juice

½ teaspoon salt

Catfish

¼ cup all-purpose flour

2 tablespoons cornmeal

¼ teaspoon salt

¼ teaspoon black pepper

¼ teaspoon paprika

¼ teaspoon garlic powder

2 tablespoons canola or vegetable oil

4 medium catfish fillets (about 1¼ pounds)

Lime wedges

Chopped fresh cilantro (optional)

*Jalapeño peppers can sting and irritate skin, so wear rubber gloves when handling peppers and do not touch your eyes.

1. To make salsa, combine cherries, red onion, jalapeño, lime juice, orange juice and salt. Stir well; refrigerate.

2. To make catfish, combine flour, cornmeal, salt, pepper, paprika and garlic powder on a dinner plate. Heat oil in large, heavy-bottomed skillet. Dredge catfish in flour mixture, coating completely. Ease into oil. Fry catfish over medium-high heat 4 to 5 minutes per side or until fish is golden brown and no longer translucent in center. Serve catfish with cherry salsa and lime wedges. Sprinkle with cilantro, if desired.

Makes 4 servings

Per Serving: 263 calories, 8.3g fat (1.5g saturated, 3.4g monounsaturated, 2.5g polyunsaturated), 92mg cholesterol, 470mg sodium, 18.3g carbohydrate (1.3g dietary fiber), 28.2g protein

Fillets with Mole Verde

Filetes con Mole Verde

Mole Verde

- 2 cups vegetable broth
- 3 large tomatillos, peeled
- ½ medium onion
- 4 garlic cloves
- 6 ounces pumpkins seeds
- 1 serrano chile
- ¾ teaspoon salt, divided
- 1 tomato
- ¼ cup cilantro

Batter

- 1 cup all purpose flour
- 2 teaspoons salt
- ½ teaspoon black pepper
- 1 egg
- 1 cup Mexican beer
- ¼ cup canola or vegetable oil
- 1 to 1½ pounds small red snapper fillets (about 6 fillets)

1. Place vegetable broth, tomatillos, onion, garlic, pumpkin seeds, serrano, ½ teaspoon salt, tomato and cilantro in blender or food processor; purée until smooth. Transfer to medium saucepan; cover and simmer on low 20 minutes.

2. Mix together flour, remaining ¼ teaspoon salt, black pepper, egg and beer in shallow bowl.

3. Heat oil in 12-inch skillet over medium-high heat. Pat dry fish fillets with paper towel. Lightly coat each fillet on both sides with flour mixture; shake off excess. Working with as many fillets as will fit in skillet in a single layer, cook 4 to 8 minutes until light brown on outside and opaque at center, turning once. Drain on paper towels; transfer to serving plate and keep warm. Repeat with remaining fillets.

4. Heat reserved sauce over medium heat, stirring frequently. Pour around fish.

Makes 6 servings

Per Serving: 398 calories, 12.4g fat (2.3g saturated, 4g monounsaturated, 4.1g polyunsaturated), 64mg cholesterol, 1654mg sodium, 46.7g carbohydrate (3.6g dietary fiber), 27g protein

Grilled Fish with Corn Salsa

Pescado Asado con Salsa de Elote

½ cup seeded and chopped tomato

¼ cup thinly sliced green onions

1 tablespoon chopped fresh cilantro

1 teaspoon fresh lime juice

½ yellow chili pepper or jalapeño pepper

½ teaspoon salt

1½ pounds halibut steaks

2 teaspoons olive oil

Salt and black pepper to taste

1 cup freshly cooked white corn ears or canned corn

Chives (optional)

1. To make salsa, combine tomato, green onions, cilantro, lime juice and jalapeño in small bowl; mix well. Season with salt. Let stand at room temperature 30 minutes to blend flavors.

2. Brush fish with 2 teaspoons oil; season with salt and pepper. Grease grill grid. Prepare grill for direct cooking. Place fish on grid 4 to 6 inches above ash-covered coals. Cook, turning once, 4 to 5 minutes on each side or until fish just begins to flake.

3. Add corn to salsa, stir to combine. Serve with salsa. Garnish with chives.

Makes 4 servings

Per Serving (halibut and salsa): 232.5 calories, 4g fat (.6g saturated, 1.1g monounsaturated, 1.6g polyunsaturated), 36mg cholesterol, 251g sodium, 22g carbohydrate (.4g dietary fiber), 26.6g protein

Orange-Glazed Salmon
Salmón Anaranjado-Esmaltado

2 tablespoons soy sauce

2 tablespoons orange juice

1 tablespoon honey

¾ teaspoon grated fresh ginger

½ teaspoon rice wine vinegar

¼ teaspoon sesame oil

Salmon

1 tablespoon butter or olive oil

4 salmon fillets (about 6 ounces each)

1 teaspoon salt

½ teaspoon ancho chile powder or paprika

1. To make glaze, whisk soy sauce, orange juice, honey, ginger, vinegar and sesame oil in small bowl; set aside.

2. Heat butter in medium nonstick skillet over high heat. Place salmon, skin side up, in skillet; brush with glaze. Cook salmon 4 minutes or until center is opaque. Carefully turn; brush with glaze. Sprinkle salmon with salt and chile powder. Cook 4 minutes. (Salmon will be slightly pink in center.) Transfer salmon to serving plate.

Makes 4 servings

Per Serving: 149 calories, 6.1g fat (2.3g saturated, 1.7g monounsaturated, 1.4g polyunsaturated), 52mg cholesterol, 491mg sodium, 6g carbohydrate (.1g dietary fiber), 17.3g protein

Oregano Garlic Clams
Almejas al Ajo y Orégano

2 pounds littleneck clams

2 teaspoons olive oil

¼ cup finely chopped onion

2 tablespoons chopped garlic

½ cup dry white wine

¼ cup finely chopped red bell pepper

1 teaspoon fresh oregano

2 tablespoons lemon juice

1 tablespoon chopped fresh parsley

1. To clean clams, scrub with stiff brush under cold running water. Discard any clams that remain open when tapped with fingers.

2. Heat oil in large saucepan over medium-high heat until hot. Add onion and garlic; cook and stir about 3 minutes or until garlic is tender but not brown. Add clams, wine, bell pepper, oregano and lemon juice. Cover; simmer 3 to 10 minutes or until clams open. Transfer clams as they open to large bowl; cover. Discard any clams that do not open. Increase heat to high. Add parsley to liquid in pan; boil until liquid reduces to ¼ to ⅓ cup. Pour over clams; serve immediately.

Makes 4 servings

Per Serving: 221 calories, 4.6g fat (.5g saturated, 1.8g monounsaturated, .8g polyunsaturated), 77mg cholesterol, 167mg sodium, 9.3g carbohydrate (.5g dietary fiber), 29.6g protein

Tequila Garlic Shrimp
Camarónes con Tequila y Ajo

2 tablespoons clarified butter*

¼ cup minced garlic

1½ pounds large raw shrimp (8 to 12 count), peeled and deveined

6 green onions, thinly sliced

¼ cup tequila

½ lemon

1 tablespoon finely chopped fresh parsley

1 tablespoon finely chopped fresh cilantro

Salt and black pepper to taste

Lemon wedges (optional)

To clarify butter, melt over low heat. Skim off white foam that forms on top, then strain clear golden butter through cheesecloth. Discard milky residue at bottom of pan. Clarified butter will keep covered in the refrigerator for up to 2 months.

1. Heat clarified butter in large skillet over medium heat. Add garlic; cook and stir 1 to 2 minutes or until soft but not brown. Add shrimp and green onions; cook 2 minutes. Add tequila; flambé. Cook until shrimp turn pink and opaque, stirring occasionally. Do not overcook.

2. Squeeze juice from lemon half on shrimp. Add chopped parsley and cilantro; season with salt and pepper. Garnish with lemon wedges.

Makes 4 servings

Per Serving: 543 calories, 13.1g fat (5.4g saturated, 2.8g monounsaturated, 2.8g polyunsaturated), 535mg cholesterol, 544mg sodium, 24.5g carbohydrate (6.1g dietary fiber), 74.2g protein

Seven Seas Soup

Siete Mares

Seafood is both delicious and nutritious. It's a good low-calorie source of many nutrients and high-quality proteins. It's also low in fat.

6 cups water

¾ cup chopped red potatoes

⅓ cup chopped celery

½ cup chopped onion

1 garlic clove, minced

1 jalapeño pepper, chopped

8 ounces tomato sauce

2 large scallops

3 ounces clams

4 ounces cooked crab legs

6 ounces halibut, large pieces

4 ounces medium to large unpeeled shrimp

4 ounces squid, cleaned and sliced

4 ounces octopus

1 tablespoon chopped fresh cilantro

½ cup chopped tomato

1 teaspoon salt

2 tablespoons lime juice

1. Place water, red potatoes, celery, onion, garlic and jalapeño in large stock pot. Simmer 15 minutes or until potatoes are tender.

2. Add tomato sauce, scallops, clams, crab legs, halibut, shrimp, squid, octopus, cilantro, tomato and salt. Simmer 5 minutes. Add lime juice and serve in large bowl.

Makes 3 servings

Per Serving: 360 calories, 4.4g fat (1g saturated, 4.4g unsaturated), 275mg cholesterol, 1600mg sodium, 26g carbohydrate (3.5g dietary fiber), 53g protein

Veracruz Style Snapper
Huachinango a la Veracruzano

2 large banana leaves

8 ounces red snapper fillets

½ cup sliced tomato

½ whole pimento, sliced

4 green olives

¼ cup sliced white onion

½ teaspoon extra-virgin olive oil

1 medium jalapeño pepper

1 teaspoon dried oregano

1 tablespoon lime juice

½ teaspoon garlic salt

1. Preheat oven to 375°F. Line baking pan with banana leaves.

2. Clean fish, removing any bones. Place fish in baking pan on banana leaves. Arrange tomatoes, pimento and olives over fish.

3. Combine onions, olive oil, jalapeño, oregano, lime juice and garlic salt in medium bowl. Pour mixture over fish. Fold over banana leaves, fully enclosing fish. Bake 15 to 20 minutes.

Makes 2 servings

Per Serving: 231 calories, 10g fat (1.5g saturated, 8.5g unsaturated), 42mg cholesterol, 795mg sodium, 12.5g carbohydrate (1.7g dietary fiber), 24.9g protein

Tip from Chef LaLa

Parchment paper may be used if banana leaves are not available.

Traditionally this recipe is made with a whole red snapper.

Colorful Bean Salad

Frijoles de Colores

Tip from Chef LaLa

To save time, look for jarred roasted red peppers.

Each half-cup serving of dry beans only costs about 20 cents, but provides 6 to 7 grams of protein.

16 ounces canned garbanzo beans

16 ounces canned kidney beans

16 ounces canned black beans

16 ounces canned corn

2 ounces canned roasted red bell pepper, diced

2 tablespoons apple cider vinegar

1 tablespoon extra-virgin olive oil

6 ounces green bell pepper, seeded and chopped

2 tablespoons finely chopped fresh cilantro

1 tablespoon finely chopped fresh Italian parsley

Rinse and drain beans, corn and peppers. Combine all ingredients in large bowl. Chill 15 to 20 minutes before serving.

Makes 16 servings

Per Serving: 123 calories, 1.6g fat (.2g saturated, 1.4g unsaturated), 0mg cholesterol, 156mg sodium, 22.7g carbohydrate (4.4g dietary fiber), 6.2g protein

Black Bean Soup
Sopa de Frijoles Negros

8 ounces dried black beans

5 cups water

4 ounces ham hocks, diced

1 teaspoon ground cumin

1 tablespoon salt

¼ teaspoon black pepper

½ cup finely chopped fresh cilantro

½ cup finely chopped white onion

1. Rinse beans. Place in large stock pot; cover with water.

2. Cook beans 2 hours, covered, over medium heat. (Add water if needed.)

3. Add ham hocks, cumin, salt and pepper. Cook 1 hour. Garnish with chopped cilantro and onion.

Makes 8 servings or 4 cups

Per Serving: 127 calories, 1.7g fat (.5g saturated, 1.2g unsaturated), 6mg cholesterol, 931mg sodium, 21g carbohydrate (5.4g dietary fiber), 8g protein

Tip from Chef LaLa
Black beans are commonly referred to as turtle beans, probably in reference to their shiny, dark, shell-like appearance. With a rich flavor that has been compared to mushrooms, black beans have a velvety texture and hold their shape well during cooking.

Queso Crêpes with Guava Syrup

Mexican Chocolate Brownie Cupcakes

Desserts

Dulce de Leche Flan

Café de Olla Ice Cream

Every meal deserves a sweet ending. Tempt your sweet tooth with our suggestions here, including a moist, delicious tres leches cake; creamy flan; crusty bread with caramel sauce; or chocolatey cupcakes.

Queso Crêpes with Guava Syrup

Crepas de Queso y Guayaba

11 ounces guava nectar

1 cup dried, unsweetened and finely chopped nectarines

1 cup all-purpose flour

2 eggs

1 cup milk

½ cup water

¼ teaspoon salt

2 tablespoons butter, softened

6 ounces queso fresco

1¼ cups orange-flavored liqueur

1. Combine guava nectar and nectarines in small saucepan. Simmer over low heat 25 minutes or until syrupy.

2. Whisk together flour and eggs in large mixing bowl. Gradually add milk and water, stirring to combine. Add salt and butter; beat until smooth. Heat lightly oiled griddle or frying pan over medium-high heat. Pour or scoop batter onto griddle, using approximately ¼ cup for each crêpe. Tilt pan in a circular motion so that batter coats the surface evenly. Cook crêpe about 2 minutes, until bottom is light brown. Loosen with spatula; turn and cook other side.

3. Sprinkle one-fourth of each crêpe with queso fresco. Fold into quarters. Transfer crêpes to warm serving plate. Flambé guava sauce and pour over crepes. Serve immediately.

Makes 6 servings

Per Serving: 340 calories, 9.7g fat (5.3g saturated, 2.9g monounsaturated, .7g polyunsaturated), 96mg cholesterol, 214mg sodium, 55.8g carbohydrate (1.9g dietary fiber), 11g protein

Tres Leches White Cake

Pastel Tres Leches

4 eggs

1 cup butter, softened

1 cup sugar

⅔ cup milk

1½ teaspoons vanilla

3 cups cake flour

¼ teaspoon baking soda

1 tablespoon baking powder

½ teaspoon salt

7 ounces fat-free sweetened condensed milk

6 ounces fat-free evaporated milk

12 ounces light whipped topping

Mixed fresh fruit (optional)

1. Preheat oven to 350°F. Grease and flour 13 × 9-inch pan.

2. Beat together eggs, butter, sugar, milk and vanilla in a large bowl. Mix in flour, baking soda, baking powder and salt. Pour into prepared pan.

3. Bake in preheated oven 35 to 40 minutes or until cake is firm to the touch. Remove cake from oven; let cool 5 minutes.

4. Meanwhile, combine condensed and evaporated milk in medium bowl. Poke holes all around the warm cake, using a wooden skewer or toothpick. Slowly pour milk mixture evenly over holes on top of cake. Let cake cool 10 to 15 minutes more to absorb liquid. Cover and refrigerate cake in pan at least 1 hour.

5. When cake is completely cooled, spread whipped topping evenly on top. Cut into pieces and garnish with fresh fruit. Keep cake covered and refrigerated.

Makes 16 servings

Per Serving: 403 calories, 12.8g fat (7.5g saturated, 3.8g monounsaturated, .7g polyunsaturated), 86mg cholesterol, 389mg sodium, 52.5g carbohydrate (.4g dietary fiber), 4.7g protein

Mexican Chocolate Brownie Cupcakes
Brownie de Chocolate Mexicano

⅓ cup butter

2 round bars Mexican chocolate

2 eggs, beaten

1 teaspoon vanilla

⅔ cup sifted all-purpose flour

½ teaspoon baking powder

¼ teaspoon salt

Café de Olla Ice Cream (see page 170), chocolate dessert topping and chopped, toasted pecans

1. Preheat oven to 350°F.

2. Fill saucepan halfway with water. Bring to a boil. Place stainless steel bowl inside saucepan to make a double boiler. Add butter and chocolate to bowl; whisk until butter and chocolate have melted. Remove bowl from heat and add eggs and vanilla. Add flour, baking powder and salt; stir well.

3. Spray standard-sized muffin pan with nonstick cooking spray. Fill 6 muffin cups about two-thirds full with batter. Bake 20 minutes or until firm in center. Serve with Café de Olla Ice Cream, chocolate topping and pecans.

Makes 6 cupcakes

Per Serving (1 cupcake): 275 calories, 21.3g fat (9.3g saturated, 8.4g monounsaturated, 2.3g polyunsaturated), 98mg cholesterol, 246mg sodium, 18.4g carbohydrate (1.2g dietary fiber), 4.8g protein

Tip from Chef LaLa

If you can't find Mexican chocolate, replace with 2 ounces unsweetened chocolate, ¾ cup sugar and 1 teaspoon ground cinnamon.

Dulce de Leche Flan
Flan de Dulce de Leche

6 eggs

2 cans (14 ounces *each*) fat-free condensed milk

2 cans (12 ounces *each*) fat-free evaporated milk

1½ teaspoons vanilla

1 cup sugar

Sweetened whipped cream and fresh mint leaves (optional)

1. Preheat oven to 350°F. Beat eggs, condensed milk, evaporated milk and vanilla in large bowl with electric mixer at medium speed until blended.

2. Place granulated sugar in medium saucepan over medium-high heat; cook until melted and golden brown. (Mixture will be very hot.) Carefully pour sugar into 8 (4-ounce) ramekins. Fill each ramekin with milk mixture; place ramekins in 15 × 11-inch baking dish. Pour hot water into dish until halfway up sides of ramekins.

3. Bake 45 to 55 minutes or until knife inserted into centers comes out clean. Let cool. Run knife around edges of ramekins to loosen flans. Invert flans onto serving plates. Garnish with whipped cream and mint.

Makes 16 servings

Per Serving: 273.8 calories, 5.1g fat (2.5g saturated, 1.7g monounsaturated, .4g polyunsaturated), 99mg cholesterol, 120mg sodium, 47.6g carbohydrate (0g dietary fiber), 9.1g protein

Tip from Chef LaLa

Flan can also be baked 60 minutes in a 9-inch pie pan.

Carrot Cake
Pastel de Zanahoria

Tip from Chef LaLa

Baking breads with fruits and vegetables has been a longstanding tradition in the panaderias (bakeries) of Mexico.

Using applesauce instead of oil in this recipe saves 1370 calories.

Cake

4 eggs

¾ cup applesauce, no sugar added

1 cup granulated sugar

¼ teaspoon ground cloves

¼ teaspoon ground nutmeg

½ cup crushed pineapple

2 teaspoons vanilla

2 cups all-purpose flour

2 teaspoons baking soda

2 teaspoons baking powder

½ teaspoon salt

2 teaspoons ground cinnamon

3 cups grated carrots

1 cup chopped walnuts

Frosting

½ cup butter, softened

8 ounces cream cheese, softened

4 cups powdered sugar

1 teaspoon vanilla

1 cup walnuts, chopped

1. Preheat oven to 350°F. Grease and flour 13 × 9-inch pan.

2. Beat together eggs, applesauce, sugar, cloves, nutmeg, pineapple, vanilla, flour, baking soda, baking powder, salt and cinnamon in large bowl. Stir to combine. Stir in carrots. Fold in walnuts. Pour into prepared pan.

3. Bake in preheated oven 30 to 40 minutes or until toothpick inserted into center comes out clean. Let cool in pan 10 minutes; turn out onto wire rack and cool completely.

4. To make frosting, combine butter, cream cheese, powdered sugar and vanilla in medium bowl. Beat until mixture is smooth and creamy. Frost cooled cake and sprinkle with walnuts.

Makes 18 servings

Per Serving: 403.1 calories, 18.7g fat (6.8g saturated, 4.9g monounsaturated, 5.8g polyunsaturated), 75mg cholesterol, 350mg sodium, 54.4g carbohydrate (1.6g dietary fiber), 7.4g protein

Per Serving (without frosting): 168.3 calories, 5.3g fat (.6g saturated, 1.3g monounsaturated, 2.8g polyunsaturated), 47mg cholesterol, 350mg sodium, 26.6g carbohydrate (1.2g dietary fiber), 4.8g protein

Café de Olla Ice Cream
Nieve de Café de Olla

3 cups whipping cream

4 egg yolks, lightly beaten

1 tablespoon instant coffee granules

½ cup plus 2 tablespoons sugar

¼ teaspoon ground cinnamon

½ teaspoon vanilla

½ cup pecans or Sweet and Spicy Cayenne Nuts (see page 85)

1. Pour 2 cups cream into medium saucepan. Whisk egg yolks and coffee granules into cream. Heat 10 minutes over low heat, stirring constantly, until mixture reaches 160°F. Mixture will thicken as it cooks.

2. Pour mixture into bowl; stir in ½ cup sugar and cinnamon until well blended. Refrigerate 2 to 3 hours or until cold. Pour chilled mixture into ice cream maker; process according to manufacturer's directions.

3. Whip remaining 1 cup cream, 2 tablespoons sugar and vanilla until stiff. Scoop ice cream into serving bowls; top with whipped cream. Sprinkle with nuts just before serving.

Makes 16 servings

Per ½-cup Serving: 221 calories, 20g fat (10g saturated, 6g monounsaturated, 1g polyunsaturated), 114mg cholesterol, 19mg sodium, 9.8g carbohydrate (.3g dietary fiber), 1.9g protein

Tip from Chef LaLa

This is a combination of a childhood favorite, Mexican fresh-churned ice cream, and an adulthood must-have, Café de Olla. Both are staples in Mexican cuisine, and both are simple decadence at its best.

Strawberries and Cream
Fresas con Crema

1 cup Mexican cream
(crema Mexicana)

2 teaspoons sugar

½ teaspoon vanilla

2 cups sliced strawberries

Fresh mint sprigs (optional)

Whip cream until almost stiff. Add sugar and vanilla; beat until cream is fluffy. Pour mixture into 4 individual cups. Freeze 1 hour. Top with sliced strawberries and garnish with mint.

Makes 4 servings

Per Serving: 151 calories, 10.3g fat (6g saturated, 0g monounsaturated, .1g polyunsaturated), 40mg cholesterol, 41mg sodium, 11.4g carbohydrate (1.7g dietary fiber), .5g protein

Tip from Chef LaLa

If you can't find Mexican cream, use crème fraîche or whipping cream.

This dessert is very popular in Mexico; there was even a popular pop band that sang a song called "Fresas con Crema." It is also served as a snack.

Easy Pineapple-Lime Sorbet
Sorbete De Limón Y Pina

4 cups cubed fresh ripe pineapple   1 teaspoon grated lime peel

¼ cup fresh lime juice

1. Arrange pineapple in single layer on large baking sheet; freeze at least 1 hour or until very firm.*

2. Combine frozen pineapple, lime juice and lime peel in blender or food processor; purée until smooth and fluffy. (If mixture doesn't become smooth and fluffy, let stand 30 minutes to soften slightly; repeat processing.) Serve immediately.

Pineapple can be frozen up to 1 month in resealable freezer food storage bags.

Makes 8 servings

Per Serving: 96 calories, .8g fat (.1g saturated, .1g monounsaturated, .3g polyunsaturated), 0mg cholesterol, 2mg sodium, 24.6g carbohydrate (2.4g dietary fiber), .8g protein

Tip from Chef LaLa

This dessert is best if served immediately, but it can be made ahead, stored in the freezer and then softened several minutes before being served.

Raspberry Cream Pie
Pastel de Crema de Frambuesa

Crust
- 1⅓ cups ground pecans
- 2 tablespoons butter, melted
- 1 tablespoon sugar
- ¼ teaspoon ground cinnamon

Filling
- ½ cup water
- 1 envelope unflavored gelatin
- ¼ cup sugar
- 1 tablespoon fresh lemon juice
- ⅛ teaspoon salt
- 1 cup heavy cream
- 2 cups fresh raspberries or 1 bag (12 ounces) frozen unsweetened raspberries, thawed

1. Preheat oven to 350°F. Combine ground pecans, melted butter, sugar and cinnamon in medium bowl. Press onto bottom and up side of 9-inch pie plate. Bake 5 to 7 minutes or until set and lightly browned. Cool completely.

2. Pour ½ cup water into medium saucepan; sprinkle with gelatin. Let stand about 5 minutes or until gelatin is softened. Add sugar, lemon juice and salt to gelatin mixture. Cook and stir over medium-low heat until sugar and gelatin are completely dissolved. Let stand about 30 minutes or until thickened.

3. Beat cream in large bowl with electric mixer at high speed until stiff peaks form. Add to gelatin mixture. Fold in raspberries. Gently spoon into prepared crust. Freeze 1 hour before serving.

Makes 8 servings

Per Serving: 334.2 calories, 26.2g fat (9.6g saturated, 11.6g monounsaturated, 3.6g polyunsaturated), 48mg cholesterol, 101mg sodium, 25.3g carbohydrate (3.5g dietary fiber), 3.2g protein

Crusty Bread with Caramel
Pan Duro con Cajeta

Caramel
- 4 cups goat's milk or cow's milk
- 1 tablespoon light corn syrup
- 1 cup sugar
- 1 stick cinnamon
- ¼ teaspoon baking soda
- 2 tablespoons water

Crusty bread
- ⅓ cup milk
- 1 cup water
- 1 cup buttermilk
- 5 to 6½ cups bread flour, divided
- 3 tablespoons sugar
- 2 teaspoons salt
- ¼ teaspoon baking soda
- 1 package (.25 ounces) rapid rise dry yeast
- ¾ cup chopped pecans

1. To make caramel, place milk, corn syrup, sugar and cinnamon stick in medium saucepan; bring to a boil and lower heat to medium. Dissolve baking soda in water in small bowl; stir into milk mixture in saucepan. Cook until mixture thickens, stirring frequently until milk is reduced to one-third of its original volume and is caramel colored. Remove cinnamon stick; set aside.

2. Warm milk, water and buttermilk in saucepan to 110°F, being careful not to overheat (overheating will kill the yeast, preventing the bread from rising).

3. Mix 3 cups flour with sugar, salt, baking soda and yeast. Add to milk mixture and mix by hand 2 minutes. Add 1 additional cup flour and beat until batter thickens (about 2 minutes). Beat in 1 additional cup flour, then knead 8 minutes on a lightly floured surface, adding additional flour as needed. Shape into a ball.

4. Place dough ball in greased bowl and cover tightly with plastic wrap. Place in warm place (80°F to 100°F) and let rise until doubled in volume (about 30 minutes). Punch down in bowl and divide into 2 halves.

5. Spray 2 cookie sheets with nonstick cooking spray. Spread each dough half onto each sheet into an oval or square shape. Indent surface of each loaf by pressing all over with fingertips. (Don't make holes.) Cover with kitchen towel and let rise in warm place until doubled in size again (about 30 minutes).

6. Preheat oven to 375°F. Indent dough again with fingertips. Bake 20 to 25 minutes until light golden brown. Cool and cut into squares. Drizzle with caramel and pecans.

Makes 24 slices

Per serving: 244.7 calories, 5.8g fat (.7g saturated, 3.2g monounsaturated, 1.5g polyunsaturated), 12mg cholesterol, 224mg sodium, 40g carbohydrate (1.6g dietary fiber), 7.2g protein

Cinnamon Custard and Fruit
Natilla con Fruta

4 teaspoons cornstarch	¼ cup sugar
¼ cup water	½ teaspoon ground cinnamon
4 cups reduced-fat (2%) milk, divided	16 fresh strawberries and blueberries
4 medium egg yolks	8 sprigs fresh mint
1 teaspoon vanilla	

1. Dissolve cornstarch in water in medium bowl. Add 2 cups milk, 4 egg yolks, vanilla, sugar and cinnamon. Whisk to combine. Set aside.

2. Heat remaining 2 cups milk in medium saucepan. Bring to a boil and lower heat.

3. Slowly stir cold milk mixture into hot milk in saucepan. Cook approximately 20 to 25 minutes until mixture thickens to the consistency of a very thick sauce.

4. Place plastic wrap directly on custard. Chill in refrigerator 2 hours (it should thicken to the consistency of custard). Serve cold with fresh fruit. Garnish with mint.

Makes 8 servings

Per Serving: 145 calories, 5.1g fat (2.3g saturated, 11.7g monounsaturated, .5g polyunsaturated), 115mg cholesterol, 67mg sodium, 19.7g carbohydrate (1.5g dietary fiber), 5.9g protein

Glossary of Terms

Achiote Dried, red seeds of annatto trees; used as seasoning and to give food deep red color. Achiote paste is made from ground seeds; has earthy flavor with hint of iodine. Used in slow-cooked sauces and stews.

Allspice Ground and dried berrylike fruit of West Indian allspice tree. Suggests combined flavors of cinnamon, nutmeg, and cloves.

Anaheim chiles [AN-uh-hime] Mild to medium-hot spice. Usually medium green, narrow and 6 to 8 inches long. Commonly stuffed or used in salsas. Sometimes labeled chiles verdes (green chiles), New Mexico chiles or Rio Grande peppers when sold fresh. Also available roasted or canned.

Ancho chiles [AHN-choh] Broad, dried chile, 3 to 4 inches long and deep reddish brown. Rich and slightly fruit-flavored; sweetest of the dried chiles. Called poblano chiles when fresh. Most often used in sauces and stews. Ground into a powder for chili and spice rubs. Pasilla chiles may be substituted.

Annatto Refers to red Indian dye made from ground pulp of the annatto tree's seeds. Also known as achiote. Paste has light musk flavor. Used more as a dye than a spice; used primarily to color oil, butter, and cheese.

Apple cider vinegar Made from apple cider, has more mild flavor than wine vinegar. Used primarily in dressings and sauces.

Árbol chiles Thin, papery, dried red chiles. Mouth-searingly hot; often sold as Chinese hot peppers.

Avocado Has leathery skin and soft, buttery flesh; yields to light pressure when ripe.

Banana leaves Used as wrapping material for barbecuing, baking, or steaming foods. Lend a hint of flavor to food they encase.

Basil, fresh Native to India. A main ingredient in Italian cooking. Used as garnish or seasoning.

Bay leaves Aromatic bay laurel leaves, usually dried. Whole, halved, or ground, gives strong, slightly bitter taste to soups, stews, and stocks.

Black beans (frijoles negros) Small beans used often as vegetarian fillings for tacos and burritos, as side dishes or in soups and stews; also known as black turtle beans.

Black pepper Black, dried and immature pepper berries. As they dry, berries turn dark and wrinkled, forming familiar whole black peppercorns with light-colored core; this makes the light particles in ground pepper. Has warm, pungent fragrance and flavor. Ground pepper comes in fine, medium, and coarse grinds.

Blood orange Sweet orange with crimson red pulp.

Bouillon Clear, seasoned soup often used as a base for heartier soups and stews. Usually made from meat, vegetables, and seasonings. Also made by dissolving bouillon cube or powder in boiling water.

Cajeta Goat's milk caramel (goat's milk mixed with sugar and cooked until it forms a brown paste). Can be made as a dessert with fruit or milk, and cooked with sugar until thick.

Cake flour High-starch flour made from soft wheat. Ideal for baking.

California chiles Mild heat flavor similar to ancho, poblano, or pasilla chiles. Also known as Anaheim chiles, New Mexico chiles, green chiles, or chilacas. Used for chiles rellenos when fresh. Can be added to casseroles, stews, soups, and sauces.

Canned tomato purée Tomatoes that have been cooked briefly and strained, resulting in thick liquid.

Canned tomato sauce Slightly thinner than tomato purée, often with seasonings and other flavorings added so ready to use in various dishes or as a base for other sauces.

Canola oil Inexpensive, low in saturated fats, has high burning point, and does not diminish or disguise flavors.

Carne asada Marinated and broiled or grilled beef.

Catfish White-fleshed, medium-firm fish, sold in fillets. Name comes from whisker-like feelers near mouth. Wild catfish often taste muddy, farmed catfish do not. Look for fresh catfish with white rather than grayish flesh.

Cayenne pepper, ground Any hot, ground red chile pepper, used as seasoning. Whole peppers are 3 to 8 inches long and ½ inch wide. Árbol chiles are closely related and may be substituted.

Ceviche Raw seafood combined with lime juice; juice "cooks" seafood by combining with its protein, firming meat, and turning it opaque. Also spelled cebiche, seviche.

Chiffonade Julienned vegetables, usually leafy herbs and greens.

Chilaquiles Spanish name means broken-up, old sombreros, referring to appearance of dish. Family-style casserole with tortilla strips, salsa, meat, and/or cheese; most often served for breakfast with eggs or grilled meats. Good way to use stale tortillas.

Chili powder Ground, dried red chiles.

Chiles negro, dried Also called pasilla chiles; one of most common Mexican chiles.

Chipotle peppers, dried [chee-POT-tleh] Smoked jalapeño peppers, also known as ahumado chiles. Dull tan, 2 to 4 inches long, and about 1 inch wide.

Chipotle peppers, canned in adobo sauce Canned with spices, vinegar, tomato sauce,

and sometimes other chiles. Use peppers, sauce, or both in recipes.

Chocolate, Mexican Block Mexican chocolate; frequently contains cinnamon, vanilla, cloves, and ground almonds.

Chorizo Spicy sausage made with pork, garlic, and chili powder. Available crumbled and in links; Mexican chorizo is sold fresh. Used in fillings and egg dishes. MIlder chorizos come from Spain and Portugal. Mexican chorizos have a variety of chiles, mealier texture, and more complex flavor. Some chorizos contain fresh herbs, making them green.

Chuck roll Cut of meat that includes shoulder blade and ribs 1 through 5 (ribs are numbered from head to tail). Roasts from chuck contain a lot of connective tissue and require moist heat cooking to become tender.

Cilantro Green herb similar in appearance to flat-leaf parsley. Also known as fresh coriander, Mexican parsley, and Chinese parsley. Sold fresh, dried, ground, or as coriander seeds. Essential to Asian and Mexican dishes. Commonly used in salsas and soups.

Cinnamon Used in sweet and savory Mexican dishes; available ground or in tightly rolled dried sticks.

Clarified butter Clear, oil-like layer that forms on top of precipitated solids when butter is melted slowly and stands without heat. Called "ghee" in India.

Cloves Small dried flower buds of an aromatic Southeast Asian evergreen. Ground cloves are used in many cakes and soups. Whole cloves are used for baked ham and mulled wines. Act as natural preservatives in pickling solutions and oils.

Coconut cream Thick, sweetened "milk" extracted from coconut flesh. Used in desserts and tropical drinks.

Condensed milk Canned, preserved milk; water content is evaporated and sugar is added. Primarily used in confectionaries and iced drinks because will not easily freeze.

Corn husks Used to wrap food (especially tamales) before cooking. If dried, will keep indefinitely. Before use, soften by soaking; use within 2 days of being rehydrated.

Cornish hens Also called Rock Cornish game hens. Weigh up to 2½ pounds and are 4 to 6 weeks old. Small amount of meat to bone; each hen is usually enough for one serving. Best broiled or roasted.

Cornmeal White, yellow, or blue varieties; available coarsely or finely ground. Also known as maize. (Never a substitute for masa harina.)

Cornstarch White powder that thickens sauces, puddings, and gravies. 1 tablespoon is equivalent to 2 tablespoons flour in thickening power and makes clearer sauce.

Cotija cheese Aged cheese with dry, crumbly texture and salty, sharp flavor. Does not melt, so used mainly as topping for tacos, beans, and enchiladas. Add to dish just before serving. Substitute with feta.

Crema fresca Thickened cream with sour taste; similar to crème frâiche. Usually made from whipping cream and buttermilk. Used as garnish. May substitute with sour cream, which is more acidic and less rich.

Crème fraîche Thickened fresh cream with sharp, tangy flavor and rich texture. Make a substitute by mixing heavy cream with uncultured buttermilk. Cover and let stand at room temperature until thickened.

Cumin (comino) Crescent-shaped, fuzzy seeds. Most often toasted and ground; some recipes call for whole seeds. Pairs well with dried chiles and Southwestern flavors.

Dry sherry Fortified wine traditionally made in southern Spain. Drink as beverage or use in sauces.

Dry white wine Palate is sharp, not sweet. Drink as beverage or use in sauces.

Dry yeast Pressed and dried until moisture content reaches 8%, which makes yeast dormant. Yeast becomes active when mixed with warm liquid. Has much longer shelf life than fresh yeast and does not need to be refrigerated. Usually sold in ¼-ounce (7-gram) foil-lined packages. Also sold in 4-ounce jars, but once opened, must be stored in refrigerator away from moisture, heat, and light.

Empanada Pastry crust filled with meat or vegetables. Traditional Christmas dish.

Enchilada Word comes from preparation of dish. Corn tortillas are dipped "in chile"; tortillas are then rolled or stacked with filling, covered with chile sauce, and baked.

English or hot house cucumber Foot-long slicing cucumber. Pricier and less flavorful than other varieties, but has smaller seeds, thinner skin, and plastic wrapping (instead of wax coating) to improve shelf life. Not necessary to peel or seed before slicing. Can substitute with Japanese or garden cucumbers, peeled and seeded.

Evaporated milk, fat-free Canned, preserved milk; water content removed through evaporation. Similar to condensed milk but not as sweet.

Fajitas "Little belts"; refers to cut of meat, not how it is served. Use marinated and grilled skirt steak or flank steak.

Fideos Thin, vermicelli-like noodles.

Flambé To serve dishes flaming by pouring spirits over food and lighting with match or stove flame.

Flan Baked caramel custard; similar to French "crème caramel" or "crème brûlée." Baked in large shallow dish; inverted when served and excess caramel used as sauce.

Flank meat/steak Triangular muscle from underside of beef flank. Can be rolled and baked with stuffing. Called London Broil when broiled, served rare, and sliced thin and horizontally.

Flour tortillas Thin, Mexican flatbread made from all-purpose bleached flour.

Fresno chiles Bright red fresh chiles, similar in appearance to ripe jalapeños. Good in salsas and ceviches. Available in fall; substitute with ripe jalapeños.

Garbanzo beans Also called ceci, chickpeas. Popular legume in Mediterranean and Mexican cuisines.

Garlic powder Ground dehydrated garlic flakes.

Garlic, Mexican Husk lined with pink and blue; sharper than white garlic.

Gelatin Protein that gels liquids. Odorless, flavorless, and colorless. Available in granular, sheet, and fruit-flavored forms.

Ginger Root traditionally grown in Asia; Mexican recipes usually call for ground, dried ginger.

Glazed Coated with liquid, such as jelly, egg wash, or chocolate to make surface smooth and shiny.

Goat cheese Also known as "chèvre." Pure white with distinctive tart flavor. Ranges from creamy and moist to dry and semi-firm.

Goat with bones Lean meat that requires moist cooking. If processed and quartered, usually comes with four legs and rib sections. Legs and ribs can be seasoned to taste and smoked or cooked over slow cooking coals. Requires frequent basting and/or laying meat in aluminum foil to retain moisture. Complimentary flavors include chiles, garlic, and onion.

Goat milk Believed to be more easily digestible and less allergenic than cow milk.

Gouda Dutch cheese with firm, smooth texture similar to Cheddar. Available young and aged.

Granny Smith apple Firm with smooth and clean skin, deep green with occasional pink blush. Test firmness by holding apple in palm of hand. (Do not push with thumb.) Should feel solid and heavy, not soft and light.

Green bell peppers Also known as sweet peppers. "Mature" when bright green but not yet ripe; flavor is sharp and acrid. If picked after changed to red, yellow, or orange, flavor will have mellowed considerably.

Guacamole Mashed avocados mixed with onions, tomatoes, garlic, chiles, and cilantro. Usually eaten as dip with tortilla chips, but also good with raw vegetables, as topping, and as filling for tacos or burritos.

Guajillo chiles, dried [gwah-HEE-yoh] Shiny-smooth, deep burnished red, pointed, long and narrow (about 4 inches by 1 inch). Tough and must be soaked longer than most dried chiles. Also

known as guaque chiles or travieso ("mischievous") chiles in reference to not-so-playful sting. Go well with chicken and pork dishes, blackberry, and apple flavors, and grassy herbs such as marjoram and thyme. New Mexico chiles may be substituted.

Guava nectar Sweet Peruvian and Brazilian fruit. Is acidic when unripe and ripens at room temperature; when ripe, has sweet aroma and bright yellow to hot pink flesh. Has many abrasive seeds. Best in sorbets, beverages, and sauces.

Habañero chiles [ah-bah-NEH-roh] Extremely hot chiles, small and lantern-shaped. Range from light green to bright orange when ripe. Used for sauces when either fresh or dried.

Halibut steaks Lean flesh of large Atlantic or Pacific flatfish.

Heirloom tomato Tomato whose seeds have been handed down from generation to generation. No genetically modified organism can be used in its production.

Hominy maíz Traditional Native American food, also known as pozole. Made of dried corn kernels that have been soaked in slaked lime to remove husks with hull and germ.

Jalapeño juice Juice from canned, pickled jalapeños.

Jalapeño pepper [hah-lah-PEH-nyoh] Named after Jalapa, capital of Veracruz, Mexico. Smooth, dark green chiles, scarlet when

ripe. Range from hot to very hot. Have a rounded tip and are about 2 inches long and ¾ to 1 inch wide. Jalapeños are popular because they are easily seeded (seeds and veins are extremely hot). Available fresh and canned. Used in various sauces and dishes; sometimes stuffed with cheese, fish, or meat. Dried and smoked jalapeños are known as chipotles.

Japanese chile Slender red dried chile 4 to 6 inches long. Similar in appearance to the Cayenne and Thai Dragon but with mild flavor.

Jícama Thick, brown-skinned root vegetable with white, low-calorie, crunchy flesh; tastes like cross between water chestnut and potato. Primarily used in salads. When eaten raw, is usually seasoned with lime juice and chili powder. Small jícamas are sweet and moist. Good source of Vitamin C and Potassium.

Kabob Meat, fish, or vegetables skewers, grilled over fire. Also spelled kabab, kebab.

Light mayonnaise Mayonnaise contains much fat; therefore, reduced-fat mayonnaise is popular among diet-conscious. Light mayonnaise contains less calories (up to 40 less per tablespoon) and fat than regular mayonnaise.

Light sour cream Made by culturing cream or milk with lactic acid bacteria. May also be made by adding rennet or nonfat milk solids. Sour cream must contain at least 18% milk fat by weight. Low-fat and light sour cream are made from half-and-half and milk.

Littleneck clams Smallest and most flavorful hardshell clams; taste salty and are slightly chewy.

Lobster Available frozen, canned, and as fresh cooked meat. When selecting live lobster, choose a lively one that flips its tail and legs, one with a rock-hard shell if possible. A 2¼- to 2½-pound live lobster will serve one amply; will serve 2 if prepared with stuffing or crumb topping.

Long-grain rice Length is 4 to 5 times its width. Light, dry grains that separate easily when cooked. Available in white and brown varieties.

Mango Fruit with peach-like taste and flowery aroma. Skin is pink, gold, and green and flesh is deep yellow and juicy. To slice, free it from flat, oval pit in large pieces. Usually eaten ripe or in salsa. Green mangoes are used in salads and chutneys.

Masa Plain, wet stone-ground dough made with Nixtamal corn kernels that have been softened in lime solution and ground. Sold prepared and unprepared. Prepared masa has been mixed with lard and salt; yields heavy, greasy dough. Also comes finely ground and dehydrated. Can be used to make tortillas and tamales.

Masa harina Instant corn flour made from uncooked corn kernels that have been ground into flour. Makes dough for tamales and corn tortillas.

Mesclun Mixture of a dozen or more wild and cultivated greens. Often stretched with herbs, flower sprigs, or bitter greens. Should be dressed very lightly with oil and vinegar so that flavor will not be masked.

Mexican chocolate Mixture of chocolate, almonds, sugar, and sometimes cinnamon and vanilla, ground together and formed into tablets. Used in desserts, chocolate beverages, and some mole sauces. For a substitute, add dash of cinnamon to bittersweet chocolate.

Mole Thick sauce made of chiles and flavored with cumin, coriander, cinnamon, nuts, seeds, and chocolate. Complex flavor is rich and smoky. Some recipes made with fresh herbs. Often used as sauce for chicken, turkey, and pork. Types of mole vary by region.

Mustard Available as seeds and dry powder. Brown and black mustard seeds may be available only in specialty stores.

New Mexico chiles Long, dried green chiles formerly known as Anaheim chiles; now grown in New Mexico. Poblanos may be substituted.

New Mexico red chiles Mild to medium hot with an earthy flavor and slightly tart with a hint of dried cherry. Often strung in ristras to dry. Used in salsas and barbecue sauces.

Nopales Paddles, or leaves, of prickly pear ("nopal") cactus. Usually firm and crunchy; smaller paddles are more tender. Taste similar to green beans. Eaten raw or cooked. Substitute with sliced green beans.

Nopalitos Cactus paddles, usually canned and pickled, cut into strips.

Nutmeg Oval-shaped, brown, wrinkled seed of nutmeg tree. Primarily used ground in sweet and savory dishes including cakes, custards, soufflés, meatballs, and soups.

Onion Biennial grown in many varieties as a table vegetable. Common varieties include strong-flavored red onion, milder yellow onion, and bland white onion.

Oregano Also called Mexican oregano or wild marjoram. Used as seasoning, particularly in sauces and soups. Grows wild in Southwest. Substitute with marjoram or sage.

Oysters Four major United States species include Atlantic, found along the East and Gulf coasts; European, flat-shelled, round oysters of the Northwest and Maine; Olympia, the half-dollar-sized oyster in the Northwest; and fruit-flavored Pacific oyster, known for its wildly scalloped shell.

Papaya Oval fruit with yellow skin, orange-yellow flesh, and many shiny black seeds in center. When slightly underripe, flesh is firm and good for relishes. Ripens at room temperature. Flesh is soft and juicy when ripe. Skin contains natural enzymes that tenderize meat and is therefore often used in marinades. Some weigh up to ten pounds, but most are mango-sized.

Paprika Spicy seasoning ground from sweet red pepper. Used in stuffings and sauces.

Pasilla chiles Dark brown, dried chiles. Long, narrow, and thin fleshed with rich, hot flavor of dried fruit and licorice. Most often ground and used in sauces. In some places ancho chiles are called pasillas. Called chilacas when fresh. Ancho chiles may be substituted.

Pasta shells (Castellane) Ridges and conch-shell shape helps trap sauces. Cook in 13 minutes.

Picadillo Filling made of beef, spices, and other ingredients.

Picante Hot, spicy.

Pinto beans Reddish-brown speckled beans that turn pink when cooked. "Frijoles" most often refers to pinto beans. Used for refried beans, chili, or purées.

Plantain Resemble bananas in size and shape but are starchier and not sweet. Used in Caribbean and South American cuisines. Most often thinly sliced and fried. Found in large supermarkets, Hispanic, and Caribbean markets. Also known as machos.

Poblano chiles, fresh [poh-BLAH-noh] Dark green chiles with rich flavor that varies from mild to snappy. Darkest poblanos have richest flavor. 2½ to 3 inches wide and 4 to 5 inches long, tapering from top to bottom in a triangle. Fresh poblanos sold in Mexican markets and many supermarkets. Peak season is summer and early fall. Also available canned. Turn reddish-brown when ripe and are sweeter than when green. Dried poblanos are known as ancho or mulato chiles. Most frequently used for chiles rellenos.

Pomegranate Fruit with many seeds surrounded by inedible flesh and tough skin. Pulp and juice surrounding seeds taste sweet and tart. Pomegranate juice is one of nature's most powerful antioxidants.

Pork neck bones Used to season soups.

Pork shoulder Primal cut that includes front leg and section at top of leg. Contains more fat than other pork cuts, which gives it flavor and tenderness and makes this cut desirable for sausage. When well-trimmed, used for lean ground pork. Also cubed or cut into strips for kabobs, stir-frys, or stews.

Pork tenderloin Tender meat of loin muscle on each side of vertebral column.

Prepared tamale masa Masa prepared for tamales.

Pumpkin seeds (pepitas) Roasted and eaten as snack or garnish. Roasted and ground to make thickening and flavoring agent.

Queso fresco Usually, combination of cow and goat milk. Tastes like mild feta and crumbles easily. Good in salads or with beans.

Radish From Latin *radix*, or "root." Root of plant in mustard family. Skin can be white, red, purple, and/or black. Can be round, oval or elongated, ½ inch wide to 1½ feet long. Most common variety in American markets is globular or oval-shaped and red-skinned, which ranges from size of small cherry to tiny orange. Flavor can be mild to peppery, depending on variety and age.

Red bell pepper Much sweeter than green bell pepper. Often roasted and used in sandwiches, pasta, or pizza.

Red cabbage Cabbage plant with compact head of reddish-purple leaves.

Red chili powder, ground Ground dried red chiles.

Red onion Medium to large onions with purplish-red skins, white flesh, and spicy, sweet flavor. Also known as Spanish onions.

Red pimento pepper Sweet heart-shaped varieties grown for canning. Used for stuffing olives and flavoring foods.

Red snapper Named for reddish-pink skin and red eyes. Flesh is firm and contains very little fat. Usually sold in the 2- to 8-pound range. Small fish are often sold whole; large snappers sold in steaks and fillets. Suitable for any cooking method. Some varieties of rockfish are sold under "Pacific snapper" and "red snapper," and a variety of tilefish is called "yellow snapper"; however, none of these are true snapper.

Refried beans (refritos) "Refried" is deceptive; "refritos" means fried, not refried.

Romaine lettuce Has long, narrow leaves and crunchy ribs. Also called Cos lettuce.

Scallion Also called green onion. Young onion with white base (not yet a bulb) and long, green leaves. Both parts are edible.

Serrano chiles [seh-RRAH-noh] Small, slightly pointed chiles, about 1½ inches long, with hot, savory flavor. While maturing, skin turns from green to scarlet to yellow. Fresh serranos can be found in Mexican markets and some supermarkets. Also available canned, pickled, or packed in oil, sometimes with carrots, onions, or other vegetables. Dried serrano chiles, also known as chiles seco, come whole and powdered and are generally used in sauces.

Sesame seeds, toasted Used as garnish worldwide. Made by stirring raw sesame seeds in frying pan over medium heat until golden brown.

Skirt steak Boneless beef cut from lower part of brisket.

Squash, Mexican Light green with dark speckles; plump and stubby. Slightly sweeter than zucchini, though zucchini can be used to substitute. Choose firm, unwrinkled squashes and cook soon after purchase. If kept too long, they become bitter.

Tamale Filling enclosed in masa, wrapped in corn husks or parchment paper and steamed.

Tamarind pods About 4 inches long with brown papery skin that covers sticky pulp, fibers, and seeds. Used to make drinks. Mixed with dried chiles in sauces and chiles. Primary ingredient in Worcestershire sauce. Also sold in dried bricks, as frozen pulp, purée, and canned paste. Sometimes called Indian dates.

Tequila, silver Pale, sharp liquor made from stem of agave plant, or maguey cactus. Made near Tequila in Jalisco, Mexico.

Tilapia fillets [tuh-LAH-pee-uh] Flesh is low-fat, sweet, fine-textured, and white, sometimes tinged with pink. Suitable for baking, broiling, grilling, and steaming. Also called St. Peter's fish or Hawaiian sun fish.

Toasting dried chiles Gives dried chiles more flavor, but great care must be taken not to burn, or chiles will taste acrid. May be toasted on dry skillet or griddle over medium heat until fragrant and slightly browned on areas that touch pan. May also be cut into strips and toasted. Frying in

oil adds stronger flavor. Remove stems and seeds either before or after toasting, but always before using chiles in recipes.

Tomatillos (tomates verdes or frescadillas) Look like small green tomatoes encased in a papery husk. Pleasantly tart. Principally used to make salsas, particularly salsa verde. Good raw but many chefs cook them briefly to enhance flavor. Substitute with small green tomatoes.

Tongue Available fresh, pickled, smoked, and corned. Can be prepared many ways, served hot or cold. Tough and requires long, slow cooking to make it tender. Beef tongues weigh 2 to 5 pounds, veal tongues ½ to 2 pounds, pork tongues about 1 pound, and lamb tongues about ¼ pound. Fresh tongue should be refrigerated no more than 1 day before cooking. Must be scrubbed thoroughly before using.

Tostada Flat, fried corn tortilla.

Veal Calf meat.

Vegetable oil Any oil from plants.

Wheat tortillas Thin disk of unleavened bread made from wheat flour and baked on hot surface.

White pepper Ground from peppercorns that have had outer black layer removed.

Yellow cornmeal See cornmeal.

Yucatán Peninsula in southeast Mexico between Caribbean Sea and Gulf of Mexico. Includes many Mayan and Toltec sites.

Index

METRIC CONVERSION CHART

VOLUME MEASUREMENTS (dry)

1/8 teaspoon = 0.5 mL
1/4 teaspoon = 1 mL
1/2 teaspoon = 2 mL
3/4 teaspoon = 4 mL
1 teaspoon = 5 mL
1 tablespoon = 15 mL
2 tablespoons = 30 mL
1/4 cup = 60 mL
1/3 cup = 75 mL
1/2 cup = 125 mL
2/3 cup = 150 mL
3/4 cup = 175 mL
1 cup = 250 mL
2 cups = 1 pint = 500 mL
3 cups = 750 mL
4 cups = 1 quart = 1 L

VOLUME MEASUREMENTS (fluid)

1 fluid ounce (2 tablespoons) = 30 mL
4 fluid ounces (1/2 cup) = 125 mL
8 fluid ounces (1 cup) = 250 mL
12 fluid ounces (1 1/2 cups) = 375 mL
16 fluid ounces (2 cups) = 500 mL

WEIGHTS (mass)

1/2 ounce = 15 g
1 ounce = 30 g
3 ounces = 90 g
4 ounces = 120 g
8 ounces = 225 g
10 ounces = 285 g
12 ounces = 360 g
16 ounces = 1 pound = 450 g

DIMENSIONS

1/16 inch = 2 mm
1/8 inch = 3 mm
1/4 inch = 6 mm
1/2 inch = 1.5 cm
3/4 inch = 2 cm
1 inch = 2.5 cm

OVEN TEMPERATURES

250°F = 120°C
275°F = 140°C
300°F = 150°C
325°F = 160°C
350°F = 180°C
375°F = 190°C
400°F = 200°C
425°F = 220°C
450°F = 230°C

BAKING PAN AND DISH EQUIVALENTS

Utensil	Size in Inches	Size in Centimeters	Volume	Metric Volume
Baking or Cake Pan (square or rectangular)	8×8×2	20×20×5	8 cups	2 L
	9×9×2	23×23×5	10 cups	2.5 L
	13×9×2	33×23×5	12 cups	3 L
Loaf Pan	8½×4½×2½	21×11×6	6 cups	1.5 L
	9×9×3	23×13×7	8 cups	2 L
Round Layer Cake Pan	8×1½	20×4	4 cups	1 L
	9×1½	23×4	5 cups	1.25 L
Pie Plate	8×1½	20×4	4 cups	1 L
	9×1½	23×4	5 cups	1.25 L
Baking Dish or Casserole			1 quart/4 cups	1 L
			1½ quart/6 cups	1.5 L
			2 quart/8 cups	2 L
			3 quart/12 cups	3 L

Notes